Household Furniture and Interior Decoration

Household Furniture and Interior Decoration

Classic Style Book of the Regency Period

THOMAS HOPE

WITH A NEW INTRODUCTION BY

DAVID WATKIN

FELLOW OF PETERHOUSE AND LIBRARIAN OF THE FACULTY OF ARCHITECTURE
AND HISTORY OF ART, UNIVERSITY OF CAMBRIDGE

DOVER PUBLICATIONS, INC.

NEW YORK

Published in Canada by General Publishing Company, Ltd., 30 Lesmill Road, Don Mills, Toronto, Ontario.
Published in the United Kingdom by Constable and Company, Ltd., 10 Orange Street, London WC 2.

This Dover edition, first published in 1971, is an unabridged republication, with minor corrections, of the work originally published in London in 1807 by Longman, Hurst, Rees, and Orme (printed by T. Bensley). The present edition includes a new Introduction by David Watkin and an additional selection of illustrations.

International Standard Book Number: 0-486-21710-8
Library of Congress Catalog Card Number: 75-132319

Manufactured in the United States of America
Dover Publications, Inc.
180 Varick Street
New York, N.Y. 10014

FIG. 1.
"Thomas Hope in Turkish Dress," by Sir William Beechey
(National Portrait Gallery, London).

INTRODUCTION

TO THE DOVER EDITION

THE PLATES in this book illustrate the interiors of Thomas Hope's London house and the furniture which he designed to adorn them. Engraved from drawings made by Hope himself, they constitute one of the most authentic and complete records in existence of English Regency design.

Thomas Hope was born in Amsterdam in 1769 of a wealthy banking family which had emigrated from Scotland towards the end of the seventeenth century. The Hopes were lavish collectors and entertainers and through the ever-increasing fortunes of their bank, Hope and Company, were able to exercise considerable influence on the national affairs of Holland. Thomas Hope's unusual background explains much about his own career. But the most remarkable feature of his early life was his extensive travelling. An almost unbelievably Grand Tour lasted from 1787 to 1795, in which year his family settled in London, having fled Holland on the arrival of the Napoleonic forces. In Spain, Italy, France, Germany, Egypt, Syria, Turkey and Greece he studied architecture and design, social manners and costume, he collected antiquities, he sketched and recorded buildings and land-scapes. Obsessed with a wanderlust and a desire to make himself the master of visual history, he sought a synthesis of all styles, of all religions: his house in Duchess Street was the fulfilment of that aim, *Household Furniture and Interior Decoration* the record of it.

He acquired his house in Duchess Street in 1799. It had been built about thirty years earlier by Robert Adam as part of the Portland Place development and was planned along rather French lines with a courtyard in front and a garden behind. In 1800 Hope enclosed the courtyard with a new wing along the street front to contain a picture gallery on the first floor. Payments to Flaxman for chimney-pieces were made in the same year and in July 1801 Lord Glenbervie already described the house as filled with "the most costly furniture." Hope was abroad from the spring of 1802 until May 1803 and on 1 February 1804 he sent out tickets of admission to sixty members of the Royal Academy which were to admit the bearer and three friends to the house between 18 February and 31 March. Some of the members resented these unsolicited invitations and complained at a Council Meeting that Hope desired their presence not "to meet Company but as professional men to publish his fine place." Hope's standing with these members was hardly improved by his publication towards the end of March of a pamphlet on Downing College, Cambridge, sharply criticising the designs made for the college by James Wyatt, President of the Royal Academy.

Despite Hope's tactlessness, perhaps even stimulated by it, curiosity about the house grew. In spite of themselves, members who took advantage of their tickets could not help feeling impressed. Thus the distinguished neo-classical architect George Dance, who visited the house in March 1804, "thought it better than He expected, & that by the singularity of it good might be done as it might contribute to emancipate the public taste from that rigid adherence to a certain style of architecture & of finishing & unshackle the Artists." Benjamin West was even more positive in his praise, declaring after his visit that it was "the finest specimen of true taste . . . either in England or in France." On the other hand, John Julius Angerstein, whose collection was to form the nucleus of the National Gallery in London, criticised its "imitation of a *barbarous taste,* not of that which is deemed classical." Sir John Soane was an admirer of the house and, indeed, his own house-cum-museum in Lincoln's Inn Fields afforded the closest parallel to it in London.

Soane's arrangement of vases in "the Catacombs" may well have owed something to Hope's example. He further echoed Hope by publishing in 1830 a handsome volume of plates and text illustrating his own house. Such self-conscious gestures are extremely rare in the history of architecture.

Influence of a different kind was less acceptable to Hope and he complained that ignorant copies were being made of his furniture. One of the reasons which encouraged him to publish his designs in 1807, together with full measurements, was to ensure that imitations of them might at least be accurately proportioned. After his marriage to Louisa Beresford in 1806 the house became known to an even wider circle of London society and during the latter part of this year Thomas must have been busy preparing the drawings for the book which would illustrate the scene of his wife's lavish entertainments. These drawings were engraved for him in the new outline style by a young architect called Edmund Aikin and by George Dawe, later court painter to Alexander I of Russia. The outline technique, so quintessentially neo-classical, had been pioneered by Flaxman in the illustrations to Dante which Hope himself had commissioned in Rome in 1793. However, the adoption of this technique for the plates in *Household Furniture and Interior Decoration* makes the representation of depth and shadow impossible and lessens the stylistic contrasts between differently designed objects, while the absence of colour further drains them of life. So it is a curiously disembodied, cold, spaceless effect that the book gives us; and Hope apologises for this in his Introduction. The reality was very different indeed. Even the title-page of the book is framed by an elaborate Turkish or Islamic border (itself a surprising choice for a neo-classical designer) of a type which Hope considered "remarkable for the play, or rather the flicker, of light and shade." Just as one "enters" the book through picturesque Turkish ornament, so the visitor to the house itself was greeted in the staircase hall by a full length portrait of Thomas Hope in Turkish dress painted by Sir William Beechey in 1798 (FIG. 1). And yet there is often a hardness about Hope's work which is not romantic. Thus, despite the Islamic border to the title-page of Hope's book, the lettering on the page itself is in an austere sans-serif type which was then in its infancy and in the introduction of which Hope must appear as something of a pioneer. This deliberate eschewing of something as agreeably familiar as the Roman serif is surely an exact parallel to the contemporary adoption of the baseless Greek Doric column in place of the Roman Doric with its base and its astragal below the capital. Indeed, as Soane was a pioneer in the introduction of Greek Doric into English architecture, so the lettering on his architectural drawings from 1789 onwards was in the sans-serif style.

The first five plates of *Household Furniture* depict the sculpture gallery, picture gallery and the Greek vase rooms. These were not in the body of the house but had been constructed by Hope inside the other three ranges of the courtyard. The next five plates show the five principal rooms as redecorated by Hope within the

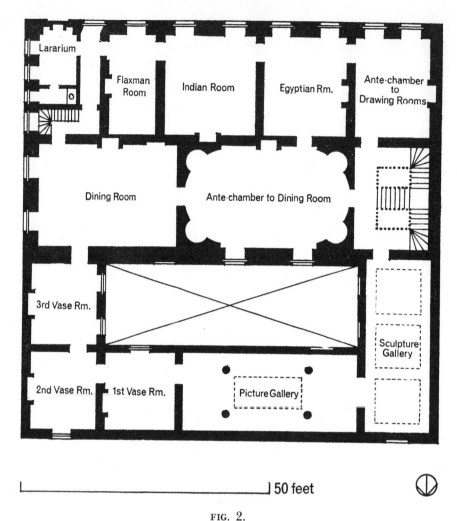

└────────────────────────┘ 50 feet

FIG. 2.
Suggested first floor plan of the Duchess Street house (drawn
by J. P. Steadman, reproduced courtesy of John Murray, Ltd.).

house itself.* All the subsequent plates illustrate individual furnishings as well as
some fine silverware made by the great Regency goldsmith, Paul Storr. One of the
strangest and most individual rooms was the Lararium, where, in a detached and
relativist manner, items representing the different religions of the world, including
Christianity, were united in terms of their romantic and artistic appeal.

The book was produced in conscious emulation of Percier and Fontaine's
Recueil de Décorations Intérieures, a dazzling record of the French Empire style
which appeared in serial form in 1801, though not in book form till 1812. A
comparison between the two books is telling. Unlike Hope, Percier and Fontaine
were obsessed by the elaboration of Roman design, not by the clarity of Greek.
Indeed, in the "Discours Préliminaire" they particularly censure the modern
adoption of the baseless Greek Doric column, whereas Hope's second plate
illustrates his picture gallery with its four noble Greek Doric columns—perhaps the
first accurate examples ever introduced into a domestic interior. Amongst Hope's
most elegant furniture are the chairs which derive from those depicted in Greek

*Figure 2 shows a suggested first-floor plan of the house (demolished in 1851), as reconstructed in
the writer's *Thomas Hope 1769–1831 and the Neo-Classical Idea* (1968), page 97.

vase paintings. Also, he blends Greek and Egyptian in a vigorous, convincing way; whereas on the rare occasions when Percier and Fontaine employ Egyptian motifs the result can be as monstrous as in the "Secrétaire servant de Bibliothèque exécuté pour M.ʳ V. à Amsterdam."

The use of animal parts, of griffins and chimaeras, lions' pads and leopards' masks, in Hope's furniture must have suggested sometimes a kind of fossilized menagerie. This "animation," however frozen, is a part of Hope's anxiety to make his furniture "speak," to make a symbolical and narrative whole of each interior. It is clear from his Introduction that his aim was "to execute, in an accurate and a classic style [objects displaying] that prodigious variety of details and of embellishments, which . . . once gave to every piece of Grecian and Roman furniture so much grace, variety, movement, expression, and physiognomy . . . ." Perhaps the most complete example of this unitive approach to interior design is the room shown in Hope's Plate 7 dominated by the marble group of Aurora visiting Cephalus on Mount Ida which Hope had commissioned from Flaxman in Rome c. 1791. "The whole surrounding decoration," Hope explains, "has been rendered, in some degree, analogous to these personages, and to the face of nature at the moment when the first of the two, the goddess of the morn, is supposed to announce approaching day. . . . The sides of the room display, in satin curtains, draped in ample folds over pannels of looking-glass, and edged with black velvet, the fiery hue which fringes the clouds just before sunrise: and in a ceiling of cooler sky blue are sown, amidst a few still unextinguished luminaries of the night, the roses which the harbinger of day, in her course, spreads on every side around her." The furniture was "chiefly gilt, in order to give more relief to the azure, the black, and the orange compartments of the hangings." Not only are the colours themselves appropriate to the theme but of course the decorative motifs reinforce the narrative. Thus there are "emblems of night . . . medallions of the god of sleep and of the goddess of night," there are owls and stars, "insignia belonging to the mistress of Cephalus . . . [and] emblems of the chace, his favourite amusement."

This personal, romantic, not to say sentimental, symbolism meant that the contemporary copies of furniture associated with it were not always wholly appropriate to their quite different settings. The furniture in the Flaxman room was, in fact, particularly popular and versions survive of the extraordinary clock (FIG. 3) and of the Jacob-inspired pier table with its figures "emblematic of the four horae or parts of the day." The architect and furniture-designer George Smith was doubtless the single most prolific imitator of Hope's work. In 1808 he published *A Collection of Designs for Household Furniture and Interior Decoration* in which not only were many of the designs derivative from Hope but also the very title of the book. Smith's plates are dated from 1804 to 1807 so it seems that as soon as the Duchess Street house was open to the public he was on the spot making careful notes and drawings. His furniture can be very spectacular but tends to be coarser and cruder than Hope's. Hope's influence at a less exotic level accounts for the popularity of the Greek "klismos" chair, of circular tables such as that in FIG. 4, cross-framed stools as in FIGS. 5 and 6, and tripod stands as in FIG. 7. Less widely imitated were his famous Egyptian chairs and couch, the strange wall lights from the Indian drawing-room (FIG. 8) and the elbow chair and startlingly original torchère shown in FIGS. 9 and 10.

Hope not only established the popularity of the types and forms of furniture mentioned in the preceding paragraph but also set his stamp on English Regency furniture by putting before the public eye numerous examples of decorative details such as winged Victories holding wreaths, colonettes with lotus leaves in the centre, and metal bolt-heads often circular or star-shaped. The frequent application of crisp ornament like gilt braid on a soldier's uniform derived ultimately from the fashionable style developed by Belanger and others in Paris in the 1780's and which was elaborated so relentlessly by Percier and Fontaine. Another aspect of Hope's design, the narrative and symbolic element, was particularly taken up by the designer Richard Brown in his book *The Rudiments of Drawing Cabinet and Upholstery Furniture . . . after the manner of the antique* (1820). Brown specifically acknowledged his debt to "Mr. Hope's mythological work on Household Furniture," to George Smith and to Percier and Fontaine, in that order. There can be no doubt that the sentimental literariness of much Victorian design grew out of the climate established by Hope and continued by Brown.

Hope's *Household Furniture and Interior Decoration* was published in May 1807 but its restlessly creative author was already looking further afield, for in the same month he purchased the Deepdene in Surrey, which he was to remodel into the most startling Picturesque country house in England. He made only one more addition to his Duchess Street house. This was the construction in 1819 of a large picture gallery to house the collection of Flemish paintings which his brother had inherited. In 1812, however, with the help of the fine Regency engraver Henry Moses, he had published *Designs of Modern Costume*. In nine of the plates in this exquisite production can be seen pieces of furniture already depicted in *Household Furniture;* and in 1823 the volume reappeared with nine additional plates under the title *A Series of twenty-nine designs of Modern Costume drawn and engraved by Henry Moses, Esq.*

The book for which Thomas Hope was best known in his lifetime was not his *Household Furniture,* but a three-volume novel entitled *Anastasius or the Memoirs of a Modern Greek, written at the Close of the 18th Century,* an exotic romance given a certain stamp of credibility by its basis in Hope's own travels in Greece and the Near East. Published anonymously in 1819, it was at first widely attributed to Byron. *An Historical Essay on Architecture . . . illustrated by Drawings made . . . in Italy and Germany* was published posthumously in two volumes and long remained authoritative, being much consulted by Ruskin. Hope's concentration

FIG. 3.
Clock (Royal Pavilion, Brighton). See Plate 7 and
Plate 13, No. 3 (of this volume).

FIG. 4.
Circular table (Victoria and Albert Museum). See Plate 39.

FIG. 5.
Cross-framed stool (courtesy of Fine Arts Engravers,
Ltd., Godalming, Surrey, and John Murray, Ltd.).
See Plate 12, No. 4.

FIG. 6.
Cross-framed chair (Royal Pavilion, Brighton). See
Plate 20, Nos. 3 and 4.

FIG. 7.
Tripod table (Victoria and Albert Museum).
See Plate 15, No. 1, and Plate 55, No. 1.

FIG. 8.
Wall lamp (Royal Pavilion, Brighton). See Plate 6.

FIG. 9.
Elbow chair (Royal Pavilion, Brighton).
See Plate 22, Nos. 5 and 6.

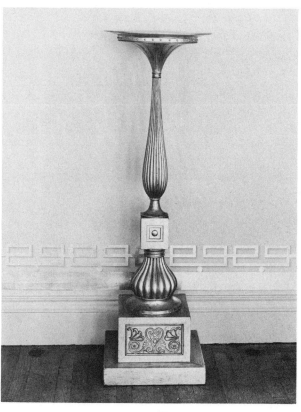

FIG. 10.
Torchère (Royal Pavilion, Brighton). See Plate 28,
No. 1.

in this book on the styles from Early Christian to Gothic shows the wide eclecticism of his tastes. Perusal of his *Costume of the Ancients** (1809)—basically a collection of plates from antique sources, particularly vase paintings—is still entertaining and instructive; though the same can hardly be said of his *Essay on the Origin and Prospects of Man* (3 vols., 1831).

Although from about 1807 onwards Hope's talents as a designer were largely employed in his experiments in the Picturesque tradition at the Deepdene, the Duchess Street mansion remained his principal home. It was in it that he died on 2 February 1831, aged only sixty-one. His body was laid to rest in the mausoleum at Deepdene which he had designed himself; within twenty years the Duchess Street mansion had been demolished and most of its contents themselves brought to Deepdene. Here they remained until 1917, when they were dispersed in two consecutive sales conducted by Messrs. Christie, Manson and Woods and by Messrs. Humbert and Flint. Thus most of the pieces depicted in *Household Furniture* survive today and many discoveries remain to be made. They will have to be reassembled, if only in the mind's eye, into a *musée imaginaire:* after all, Sir George Beaumont had described the Duchess Street mansion as early as 1804 as "more a *Museum* than anything else."

DAVID WATKIN

Peterhouse, Cambridge

STUDIES OF FURNITURE DESIGNED BY THOMAS HOPE

Harris, J., *Regency Furniture Designs*, 1961.

Honour, H., *Cabinet Makers and Furniture Designers*, 1969.

Jourdain, M., *Regency Furniture*, revised by Ralph Fastnedge, 1965.

Musgrave, C., *Regency Furniture*, 1961.

Symonds, R. W., "Thomas Hope and the Greek Revival," *Connoisseur*, CXL, 1957.

Watkin, D., *Thomas Hope 1769—1831 and the Neo-Classical Idea*, 1968.

Wellesley, Lord Gerald, "Regency Furniture," *Burlington Magazine*, LXX, 1937.

*Reprinted by Dover in 1962 with the title *Costumes of the Greeks and Romans.*

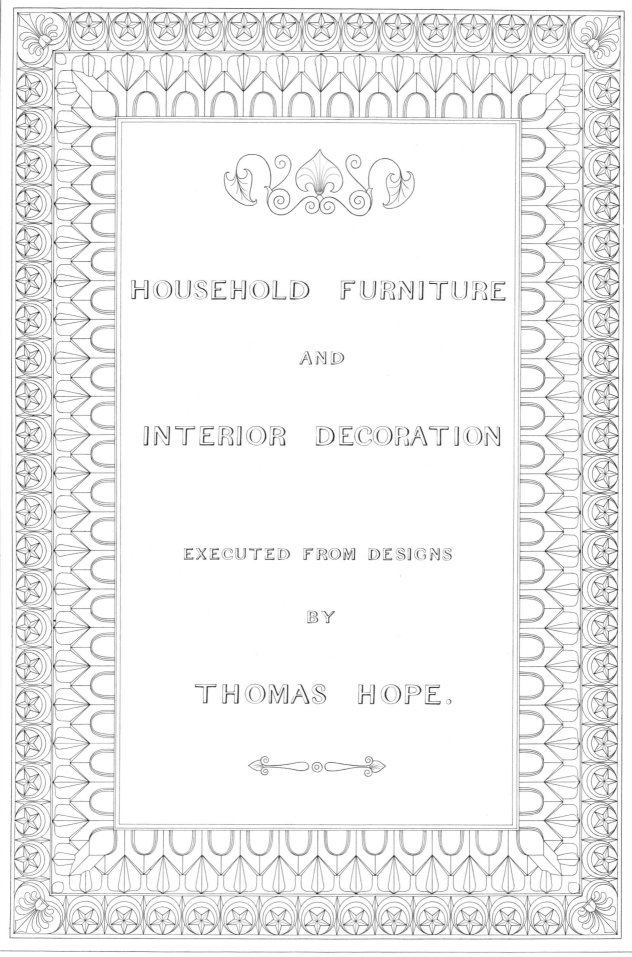

HOUSEHOLD FURNITURE

AND

INTERIOR DECORATION

EXECUTED FROM DESIGNS

BY

THOMAS HOPE.

London, Published May 1st 1807, by Longman, Hurst, Rees, & Orme, Paternoster Row.

INTRODUCTION.

UNDER the general denomination of Houfehold Furniture are comprifed an infinite variety of different productions of human induftry, wrought in wood, in ftone, in metal, in compofition of various defcriptions, in filk, in wool, in cotton, and in other lefs ufual materials. Each of thefe different articles, however fimple be its texture, and however mean its deftination, is capable of uniting to the more effential requifites of utility and comfort, for which it is moft immediately framed, and with which it can confequently, on no account, difpenfe, a certain number of fecondary attributes of elegance and beauty, which, without impeding the chief purpofe of the object, may enable its fhape and acceffories to afford additional gratification, both to the eye and to the imagination.

Almoft every one of thefe various articles however, abandoned, till very lately, in this country, to the tafte of the fole upholder, entirely ignorant of the moft familiar principles of vifible beauty, wholly uninftructed in the fimpleft rudiments of drawing, or, at moft, only fraught with a few wretched ideas and trivial conceits, borrowed from the worft models of the degraded French fchool of the middle of the laft century, was left totally deftitute of thofe attributes of true elegance and beauty, which, though fecondary, are yet of fuch importance to the extenſion of our rational pleaſures. Furniture of every deſcription, wrought by the moſt mechanical proceſſes only, either remained abſolutely void of all ornament whatever, or, if made to exhibit any attempt at embelliſhment, offered in its decoration no approach towards that breadth and repoſe of ſurface, that diſtinctneſs and contraſt of outline, that oppoſition of plain and of enriched parts, that harmony and ſignificance of acceſſories, and that apt accord between the peculiar meaning of each imitative or ſignificant detail, and the peculiar deſtination of the main object, to which theſe acceſſories belonged, which are calculated to afford to the eye and mind the moſt lively, moſt permanent, and moſt unfading enjoyment. The article only became, in conſequence of its injudicious appendages, more expenſive, without becoming more beautiful; and ſuch remained the inſipidity of the outline, and the unmeaningneſs of the embelliſhments, even in the moſt coſtly pieces, that generally, long even before the extreme inſolidity and flimſineſs of their texture could induce material injury in them from the effects of regular wear and tear, the inanity and tameneſs of their ſhapes and appendages already completely tired the eye and mind; and left theſe no other means to eſcape from the wearineſs and the diſguſt which they occaſioned, than an inſtant change for other objects of a more recent date and a more novel conſtruction. Thus all thoſe ſums and all that labour were waſted upon ever varying objects of tranſient whim and puerile faſhion, which, by being employed in the formation and in the purchaſe of objects of lafting perfection and beauty, might have increafed in endlefs progrefs the opulence of the individual, and the wealth of the community.

If any one felt a defire to decorate his habitation with furniture of fuperior elegance of form and of defign, unable, from the unfrequency of the demand, and from the confequent inability of the artificer, to get any fuch wrought at home, he was obliged to procure it from abroad. Often, at a great expenfe, he would only obtain the refufe of foreign manufactures; and even, where he fucceeded in importing the choiceft productions of continental induftry, thefe only ferved to difcourage our own artifts, to diminifh the balance of trade in our favour, and, by a tacit acknowledgment of our inferiority in the arts of elegance and tafte, to raife the pride of foreigners at our expenfe.

Thefe circumftances I beheld with regret; and, having occafion, a few years ago, to appropriate a little repofitory for the reception of a fmall collection of antiquities, Grecian and others, I determined to make a firft attempt towards giving the few articles of furniture, required for this purpofe, in addition to the more effential modifications of utility and of convenience, fome of thefe fecondary attributes of elegance and of beauty which, without being equally indifpenfable with the former, were neverthelefs conducive, not only towards rendering each feparate piece of furniture, individually, a more pleafing and a more graceful object, but above all, towards forming the entire affemblage of productions of ancient art and of modern handicraft, thus intermixed, collectively, into a more harmonious, more confiftent, and more inftructive whole.

I could not help flattering myfelf that that firft deviation from the prevailing ftyle of furniture, which I thus purpofed, would, fome time or other, produce fruits more important and more gratifying than the mere trifling and felfifh fatisfaction which I might reap from having given a fomewhat greater degree of elegance, than was ufual, to my own fingle habitation. I hoped that the change, in all thofe varied implements of ufe and comfort which every houfe of any fize requires, from a tirefome and monotonous infignificance of form and ornament, to a delightful and varied fignificance of fhape and embellifhment, of which I could only fet the example in an humble and a reftricted way, would gradually, by others, be extended to an infinitely greater number and diverfity of objects; that thus infenfibly the arts of defign, applied to every article, and ftudied in every profeffion conducive to the comforts of man, would be made to diffufe their beneficial influence throughout the minuteft ramifications even of what had hitherto been confidered as the exclufive province of the mere mechanic trades; and that confequently almoft every production of induftry, refcued in fome meafure from the hands of the mere plodding artifan, would be enabled to give fome fcope to the talent of the profeffor of the more liberal arts; the draughtfman, the modeller, the painter, and the fculptor.

Thus I hoped to afford to that portion of the community which, through the entire fubftitution of machinery to manual labour, in the fabrication of many of the moft extenfive articles of common ufe, had for ever loft the inferior kinds of employment, a means of replacing the lefs dignified mode of fubfiftence of which it had been deprived, by a nobler fpecies of labour; one which abfolutely demands the cooperation of thofe higher intellectual capacities which the former often allows to remain dormant, or even tends to extinguifh; and one in which, confequently, the powers of mere machinery never can emulate, or fupplant the mental faculties of man. Thus I hoped to open to ingenuity a new and boundlefs field, in which the greater number of artifts, who though qualified to rife above the fphere of the mere artifan, yet are not fufficiently gifted to reach the higheft provinces of the fine arts, might find an ample fource of fuch employment as, without being of the moft exalted defcription, were yet, to a certain degree, elegant and dignified; and in which, moreover, that fmaller number of fuperior men, deftined by the liberality of nature to afpire at eminence in the higheft and nobleft branches of the fine arts, might find a means firft to difcover the latent germs of their genius to themfelves and to others; firft to cultivate and to extend their abilities; firft to give to a diftruftful public earnefts of the far greater height to which more ample encouragement might ultimately carry their powers; and firft to prefent to that public inducements to beftow on them that greater encouragement required for this purpofe.

Thus I hoped to entice the wealthy, through the more general diffusion of the charms of art, and through the thence resulting more general initiation into the mysteries of taste, to divert the employment of a larger portion of their opulence from an idle and a ruinous waste of those articles of grofs sensuality or trivial amusement, which, incapable of being enjoyed until they are consumed, are only produced in order to be again destroyed, to the more profitable as well as more dignified procurement of those monuments of visible elegance and intellectual beauty which, capable of being enjoyed during the longest periods, and by the greatest numbers, without suffering any material degradation, can alone become instruments of universal and of durable gratification, as well as of solid and permanent grandeur: and thus, moreover, by enabling the lover of elegant refinement to find at home those objects of superior design and execution, which formerly he could only obtain from abroad; by converting into lucrative articles of home-manufacture, and of beneficial exportation, those very commodities which had heretofore only appeared in the repulsive and unpatriotic shape of expensive articles of foreign ingenuity and of disadvantageous importation, I hoped to increase in a considerable degree the internal resources and the external independence of the commonwealth.

Thus, in fine, I hoped to contribute my mite not only towards remotely giving new food to the industry of the poor, but new decorum to the expenditure of the rich; not only towards ultimately increasing the welfare and the commerce of the nation, but refining the intellectual and sensible enjoyments of the individual; and thus, through the distant but powerful operation of the new stimuli applied to the human mind, I flattered myself with some day seeing the same copious source of benefit here first opened, produce farther advancement in virtue and patriotism, as well as farther progress in opulence and enjoyment; farther claims to respect in our own eyes, as well as farther titles to consideration in the eyes of foreigners.

If thus great were the advantages which the adoption of the totally new style of decoration here described seemed to promise, the difficulties with which its execution was to be attended appeared not less considerable. The union of the different modifications of visible and intellectual beauty which were desirable, with the different attributes of utility and comfort which were essential; the association of all the elegancies of antique forms and ornaments, with all the requisites of modern customs and habits, having heretofore been so seldom attended to, in objects of common and daily use, I found no one professional man, at once possessed of sufficient intimacy with the stores of literature to suggest ideas, and of sufficient practice in the art of drawing to execute designs, that might be capable of ennobling, through means of their shape and their accessories, things so humble in their chief purpose and destination as a table and a chair, a footstool and a screen.

I was thus obliged to depend in a great meafure on my own inadequate abilities for the accomplifhment of my pur-pofe; and to employ that feeble talent for drawing which I had thus far only cultivated as the means of beguiling an idle hour, in the more laborious tafk of compofing and of defign-ing every different article of furniture, which I wanted the artifan and the mechanic to execute. I need not point out the arduoufnefs of the undertaking, when it is recollected that the ftyle of embellifhment which I wifhed to introduce, required in turn the application of every form of the inani-mate and of the animated creation, from the fimpleft of thofe which mark the humbleft of vegetables, the reed, the lotus, or the thiftle, to the moft complex of thofe which diftin-guifh the human frame in all its greateft ideal perfection and beauty.

Nor were the difficulties limited to the fole procefs of forwarding the requifite drawings. The leaft complicated and the leaft fignificant of fhapes, borrowed from the mere inani-mate creation, as foon as they are to prefent a rounded and an evanefcent contour, cannot be executed in relief from mere lines traced on a flat furface, however accurately thefe lines be drawn, with any degree of precifion and truth; ftill much lefs can the infinitely more complicate, more fignificant, and confequently more beautiful forms, borrowed from animated nature, which every where uniformly difplay this evanefcent and receding outline, be transferred to the relief, from fuch a flat furface, with the exactnefs and the nicety required by ornaments of this high ftamp, in order not to be converted, from the nobleft of decorations, into the moft difgufting of deformities. From the lines firft traced by the draughtf-man, on a mere plane, muft ftill, in the fecond place, by the modeller, be wrought, in fome foft and yielding fub-ftance, a rilievo, exhibiting in detail all thofe projections and receffes, which are unfufceptible of being expreffed in the drawing, and which neverthelefs are intended to be difplayed in the actual implement, before thefe concavities and thefe convexities can, in the third and laft inftance, by the carver or the cafter be, with any certainty of fuccefs, transferred to the more folid and more inflexible material, out of which the utenfil itfelf is finally to be wrought: and, if I had in vain fought a fpecies of defigners, ftill lefs was I able to find a defcription of modellers, fufficiently familiar with the various productions of art and of nature, with the coftume of ancient times, and with the requifites of modern life, with the records of hif-tory, and with the allufions of mythology, to execute, in an accurate and a claffic ftyle, that prodigious variety of details and of embellifhments, which, under the various characters and denominations of imitative and of fymbolic perfonages, of attributes and of infignia of gods and of men, of inftru-ments and of trophies, of terms, caryatides, griffins, chi-mæras, fcenic mafks, facrificial implements, civil and mili-tary emblems, &c. once gave to every piece of Grecian and Roman furniture fo much grace, variety, movement, expref-fion, and phyfiognomy; fo much wherewithal to afford to the eye and the mind the moft luxuriant and uncloying treat.

Thence I found myfelf under the neceffity of procuring, with great trouble, and ftill greater delay, models and cafts from Italy, for almoft all the leaft indifferent compofitions which I have had executed; and under the ftill more painful neceffity of abandoning the execution of many, in my opinion, far happier and more pleafing ideas, than thofe which I fucceeded in bringing to light, from the utter impoffibility of obtaining, in any way whatever, the requifite models.

Like the race of draughtfmen and of modellers, that of carvers in wood and ftone, and of cafters in metal and compofition, who, without being qualified to take rank among the profeffors of the higher branches of the liberal arts, the ftatuary and the painter, might ftill poffefs abilities to execute objects of elegance, fomewhat foaring above the commoneft picture frame or pier table, and the commoneft grate or ftove, were almoft totally wanting. Throughout this vaft metropolis, teeming as it does with artificers and tradefmen of every defcription, I have, after the moft laborious fearch, only been able to find two men, to whofe induftry and talent I could in fome meafure confide the execution of the more complicate and more enriched portion of my defigns; namely, Decaix and Bogaert: the firft a bronzift, and a native of France; the other a carver, and born in the Low Countries. And I need not add how flow and tedious this fcarcity of workmen has rendered the completion of my little collection.

Under thefe numerous obftacles and difficulties, I have hitherto been able to make but very little progrefs in my attempts at improvement on the generally prevailing tafte of decoration. I have hitherto fucceeded in embodying in wood and metal, in imprinting in paper and on cotton, but a very fmall portion of the later and more extended ideas which, in the courfe of my firft and more reftricted endeavours, I fucceffively was led to conceive.

Still, perceiving (and with unfeigned pleafure) that even thefe few earlieft attempts at a melioration of tafte, rude and imperfect as they neceffarily remained in their modifications, had neverthelefs already met with fufficient approbation from the public at large, to induce feveral profeffional men, upholders, cabinet-makers, and others, to abandon in fome degree the old beaten track, fo long unremittingly purfued, and to attempt exhibiting, either in reality or in engravings, not only a general approximation to the ftyle for which I wifhed to introduce a tafte, but frequently a direct imitation of the individual objects, of which I had planned the defigns for my own exclufive ufe, I thought it might prove neither totally unacceptable nor totally ufelefs, to publifh of thefe various articles fome geometrical and other views, fufficiently faithful and detailed to prevent a hafty furvey of the originals from producing, inftead of judicious imitations, extravagant caricatures, fuch as of late have begun to ftart up in every corner of this capital, and fuch as, by exhibiting the different fpecies of ornament of which I have endeavoured to prefent fpecimens, moft wretchedly diftorted, moft injudicioufly applied, and moft inconfiftently united, feem calculated for the fole purpofe of bringing this new ftyle into complete difrepute with thofe who, uninclined to give themfelves the trouble of diftinguifhing between a new original and the paltry copies which it never fails to produce, envelope in the fame general undifcriminating cenfure and obloquy whatever their eyes have not been accuftomed to behold, or their mind to comprehend.

Even this latter object however, namely, the faithfully reprefenting the various articles which I had had executed, was not as eafily accomplifhed as might, at firft fight, be imagined.

The mode of engraving beft calculated to render the effect, and to facilitate the imitation of objects, whofe chief merit confifts in the chaftity and the play of their contour, is in mere outlines. This fpecies of engraving however, which allows no blending tints of light and fhadow, introduced in the body of the object reprefented, to remedy any uncertainty, to palliate any tamenefs, or to glofs over any imperfection that may have been left in the everywhere equally fenfible, equally undifguifed outline, and which confequently requires in the engraver all the maftery of the practifed draughtfman, had been woefully neglected in this country, where in general engravers, contenting themfelves with copying the productions of painters by mere rule and compafs, poffefs not themfelves, in the nobler art of drawing, any accuracy of eye and freedom of hand.

Under thefe circumftances it was impoffible to meet, in the line of engravers, with an artift, ready formed, by prior practice, to treat with fpirit in fimple outlines, objects fo new to the graver, fo different from thofe heretofore exhibited in copper-plate, as the implements and the decorations in quef- tion; with one who underftood giving to the numberlefs va- rieties of foliage and of figures, which adorn every part and enliven every detail, all that truth of nature, and all that fe- lection of art, all that real and all that ideal perfection, all that correctnefs and all that grace, which fo effentially belong to the beft antique performances, and to thofe modern works that profefs to retrace their various excellencies.

Even where the germs of the peculiar fpecies of abilities, requifite for this purpofe, happened to exift, they ftood in need of a total new development, as yet unaccomplifhed, be- fore the artift might be faid to be formed; and I flatter my- felf that the infpection of my work, and the comparifon be- tween fome of its earlier engravings and others of a later date, will fhew that this very collection, trifling as it may appear, has not been entirely unproductive of the beneficial effect of cultivating a new defcription of art, fo urgently wanted, and hitherto fo rarely poffeffed. At leaft I cannot fpeak too highly in this refpect of the exertions of Mr. Aikin and of Mr. Dawe, to whofe affiftance I am chiefly indebted for the completion of the plates which I here fubmit to the public.

Still could not, under all the exifting circumftances, the moft fanguine difpofition flatter me with hopes of producing in London a work at all comparable, in point of elegance of defigns and of excellence of execution, with that publication which at prefent appears at Paris on a fimilar fubject, directed by an artift of my acquaintance, Percier, who, having profeffionally devoted the firft portion of his career to the ftudy of the antique chef-d'œuvres in Italy, now devotes the latter portion of his life to the fuperintendance of modern objects of elegance and decoration in France; and who, uniting in himfelf all the different talents of the antiquarian, the draughtf-man, the modeller, and the engraver, has not only been enabled to invent and to defign the moft beautiful articles of furniture, of cabinet-work, and of plate, but has ftill been able, in many of the etchings which he himfelf has made from his compofitions of this defcription, to improve, through the freedom and the gracefulnefs of his touch, on the merit of the original drawings; whereas, under a ftrange and a lefs fkilful hand, the fpirit of the originals muft have entirely evaporated in the reprefentation.

The impoffibility, however, under which I felt myfelf, of rendering the execution of my work adequate to the higheft ideal which I might conceive, did not appear to me a fufficient motive for withholding a performance which, without being reckoned fuperlatively excellent, might yet, perhaps, be thought more or lefs ufeful; and I determined on ufhering into light the prefent collection of plates, fuch as it was, in hopes that an indulgent public would make fome allowance for its imperfections, in confideration of the many difficulties which prevented its receiving a greater degree of excellence.

The work might, perhaps, have been rendered more copious and more fhewy, by offering, in addition to the reprefentations of fuch pieces of furniture as actually have been executed, the defigns of fuch other more gaudy and more fplendid articles of decoration, as hitherto could only have been fubmitted in the character of mere projects for future execution; but I thought that the collection would remain more deferving of reliance and of imitation, more fecure from the objections fo eafily ftarted againft the practicability of whatever has not yet been actually put in practice, by being exclufively confined, in its reprefentations, to objects whofe effect had already been tried, and had been approved of.

I beg however to obferve that, though in general this effect is beft rendered, on paper, by a mere lineal engraving, this circumftance is not univerfally the cafe. In many ornaments, either very boldly projecting, or very deeply receding, much of the beauty muft depend on the ftrong contraft of the light and of the fhaded parts. In many other fpecies of decoration, deftitute of ftrong relief or chiaro-fcuro, fome part of the elegance muft be founded on the harmonious blending, or the gay oppofition of the various colours. Neither of thefe different fpecies of merit could have been expreffed with any fuccefs in my work, otherwife than by enhancing its price to fuch a degree as muft have defeated its principal purpofe.

In England much more attention is generally paid to the perifhable implements of the ftable than to the lafting decoration of the houfe; and it is therefore not impoffible that many, even among thofe moft difpofed yearly to lavifh enormous fums in the trifling and imperceptible changes which every feafon produces in the conftruction of the tranfient vehicle, may moft ftrongly object to the expenfivenefs of the infinitely more important and more palpable improvements, of which is fufceptible the more permanent fixture. To fuch it would be eafy to prove, that the mode of decorating apartments, hitherto in vogue, which, through the paltrinefs of its materials, and the flightnefs of its texture, is fubject to experience fuch fpeedy decay, and (what is worfe) through the poverty of its forms, and the unmeaningnefs of its embellifhments, is liable to occafion fuch rapid difguft; and which, confequently, is ufually broken or difcarded, long ere it has had leifure fairly to ferve its time, though at firft its coft be lefs, yet, by means of the inceffant change of fafhion which it ftimulates and fupports, on the whole, occafions a much greater expenfe than the ftyle of furniture here fet forth; which, little fufceptible of experiencing premature deftruction, for want of due folidity of form, and lefs liable, it is prefumed, than the former, to fuffer merited difgrace, while yet in all its frefhnefs of youth, for want of intrinfic power to pleafe, may be preferved in families, from generation to generation, as a valuable portion of the patrimonial eftate.

Had this work been more meritorious than I have been enabled to render it, ftill fhould I have urged the young artift, into whofe hands it may fall, as I now do, moft ftrenuoufly, to confider it as publifhed rather with the view to give a vague idea of what has, hitherto, with imperfect means, been reftrictedly and haftily effected, in a new line of induftry and tafte, than with the intention of offering fpecific models of what fhould, in future, by greater ftudy and application, be, in this new line, more extenfively and more permanently executed: ftill fhould I have warned him moft earneftly againft confining his exertions to a mere fervile copying of the contents of this volume.

Such a proceeding as that againft which he is here cautioned, could only make him continue to move, as he has too much done heretofore, in an eternal round of undeviating famenefs. To emerge from this fervile track, to take a higher flight, he fhould not ftop his progrefs at the ftudy of my humble publication; he fhould afcend to thofe higher, thofe more copious fources of elegance, whence I myfelf have drawn all my ideas, and which alone can offer an inexhauftible ftore of ever varied and ever novel beauties. I mean, in the firft place, thofe productions of Nature herfelf, animate or inanimate, which contain the firft elements and the firft models of all the perfections of art; and, in the fecond place, thofe monuments of antiquity which fhew the mode in which the forms of nature may be moft happily adapted to the various exigencies of art.

I fhall now proceed to give a fhort explanation of the chief contents of each Plate: here and there fubjoining to this account fuch few additional obfervations, fuggefted by the objects defcribed, as I think may be of moft general utility.

EXPLANATION.

THE border which furrounds the title-page is copied from the frame of a picture, reprefenting a Turkifh perfonage. The mouldings of this picture-frame offer an imitation of a fpecies of ornament, refembling congelations and ftalactites, which feems to owe its invention to the Grecian architects of the lower empire, and which is remarkable for the play, or rather the flicker, of light and fhade, which it derives from the fharpnefs of its multifarious angles, and from the re-flexion of its numerous facets. At Conftantinople this fingular and not inelegant fpecies of ornament adorns, in an infinite variety of modification, the capitals, the entablatures, the niches, and the gateways, of moft of the Greek churches and Mohammedan mofques, defigned by Grecian builders. From that principal feat of arts and of refinement, during the middle ages, its fafhion feems to have extended in every direction, throughout Europe, Afia, and Africa. It forms a confpicuous feature in almoft all the fplendid Saracenic monuments of Arabia, of Egypt, and of Perfia. Weftward it reached as far as Spain, where it adorns the palaces of the Alhambra and of the Generalifa at Seville, and the mofque at Cordova; and eaftward it travelled as far as India, where it decorates every Moorifh building of any importance. Even in the north of Europe fome rude imitations of this ornament are difcernible in the facred and other ftructures, known by the name of opus Romanum; that offspring of the already corrupt Grecian architecture which prevailed at Conftantinople, ftill more degenerate than its parent. In England the copy of the earlier and fimple modifications of this fpecies of ornament may be traced, under the appellation of zig-zags, of chevrons, of billets, &c. in moft of the oldeft cathedrals whofe architecture has, till very lately, improperly been denominated Saxon.

A profile of this picture-frame is given in the Plate 53, No. 1, but it fhould be obferved that, from the circumftance of the varied projections and receffes which its mouldings offer, floping in every direction, their profile muft be different in every point of fpace which intervenes between each periodical return of the fame forms.

PLATE I.

STATUE GALLERY.

As this room is deſtined ſolely for the reception of ancient marbles, the walls are left perfectly plain, in order that the back-ground, againſt which are placed the ſtatues, might offer no inferior ornaments, or breaks, capable of interfering, through their outline, with the contour of more important works of art. The ceiling admits the light through three lanterns, and is divided into caſſoons by means of rafters, which imitate a light timber covering.

PLATE II.

PICTURE GALLERY.

In this room the center part of the ceiling is fupported by fmall columns, which divide the lights, and which are imitated from thofe that are feen at Athens, in the upper divifion of the octagon building, vulgarly called the temple of the Winds. Thefe columns reft on maffy beams, fimilar to thofe in marble, which lie acrofs the periftyle of the temple of Thefeus, alfo at Athens. The larger columns which fupport the entablature offer the profiles of thofe of the Propylæa.

Along each fide of this room extends a cornice, from which are fufpended curtains, deftined occafionally to protect from the fun the feveral compartments of pictures, hung againft the walls; and thefe curtains are here reprefented as actually let down over the pictures.

At the farther end of this gallery ftands an organ, the Ionic order of whofe columns, entablature, and pediment, has been copied from the exquifitely beautiful fpecimen difplayed in the temple of Erectheus, in the Acropolis of Athens. The car of the god of mufic, of Apollo, glides over the center of the pediment. The tripods, facred to this deity, furmount the angles. Laurel wreaths and other emblems, belonging to the fon of Latona, appear embroidered on the drapery, which, in the form of an ancient peplum or veil, defcends

over the pipes of the inftrument, and gives it the appearance of a fanctuary.

Large tables, deftined for portfolios of drawings and books of prints, occupy the middle of this gallery, and a few antique implements and remains are placed along its fides.

PLATE III.

ROOM CONTAINING GREEK FICTILE VASES.

As thefe vafes were all found in tombs, fome, efpecially of the fmaller fort, have been placed in receffes, imitating the ancient Columbaria, or receptacles of Cinerary urns. As they relate chiefly to the Bacchanalian rites, which were partly connected with the reprefentations of myftic death and re-generation, others, of a larger fize, have been fituated in compartments, divided by terms, furmounted with heads of the Indian or bearded Bacchus.

PLATE IV.

SECOND ROOM CONTAINING GREEK VASES.

The ſcenic maſk, the Thyrſus, twined round with ivy wreaths, the panther's muzzle and claw, together with other inſignia of Bacchus, decorate in ſeveral places the furniture of this room. A range of rounded reeds ſupports the lower tier of ſhelves; ranges of ſquare rafters ſuſtain the two upper tiers.

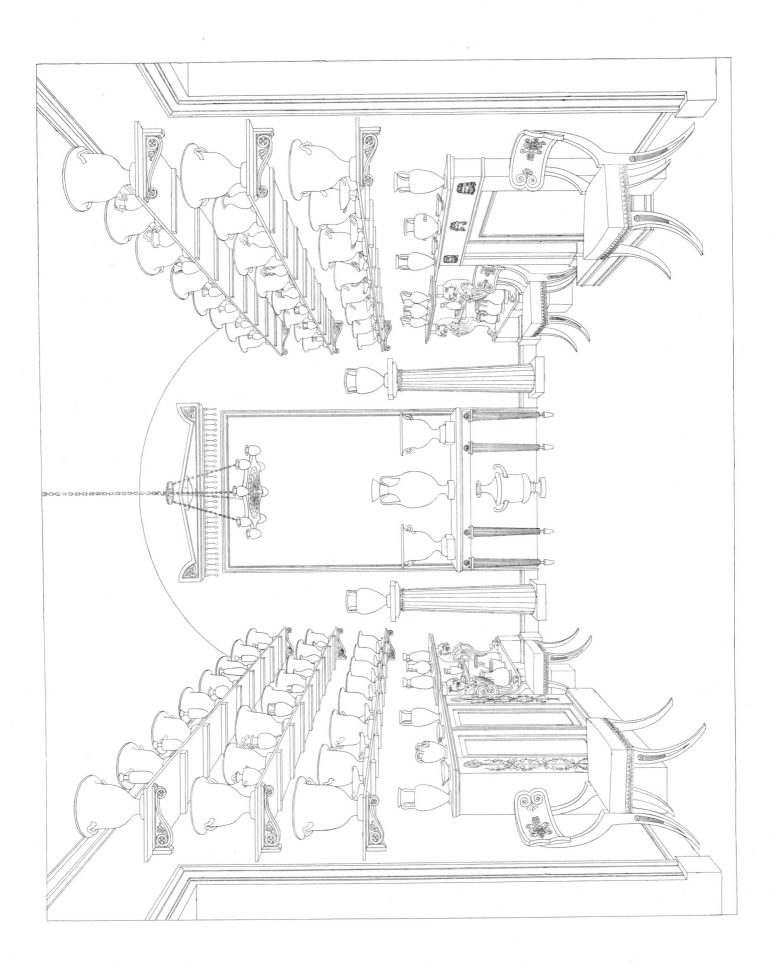

PLATE V.

THIRD ROOM CONTAINING GREEK VASES.

A table fupported by chimæras in bronze, fimilar to fome limbs of ideal animals, adapted to the fame purpofe, which have been found among the remains of Pompeia; a bronze lamp, bronze candelabra, and a few other utenfils, of a quiet hue and of a fepulchral caft, analogous to the chief contents of this room, form the principal ornaments which accompany the vafes.

PLATE VI.

DRAWING-ROOM.

This room was principally fitted up for the reception of four large pictures, executed by Mr. Daniel, and reprefenting

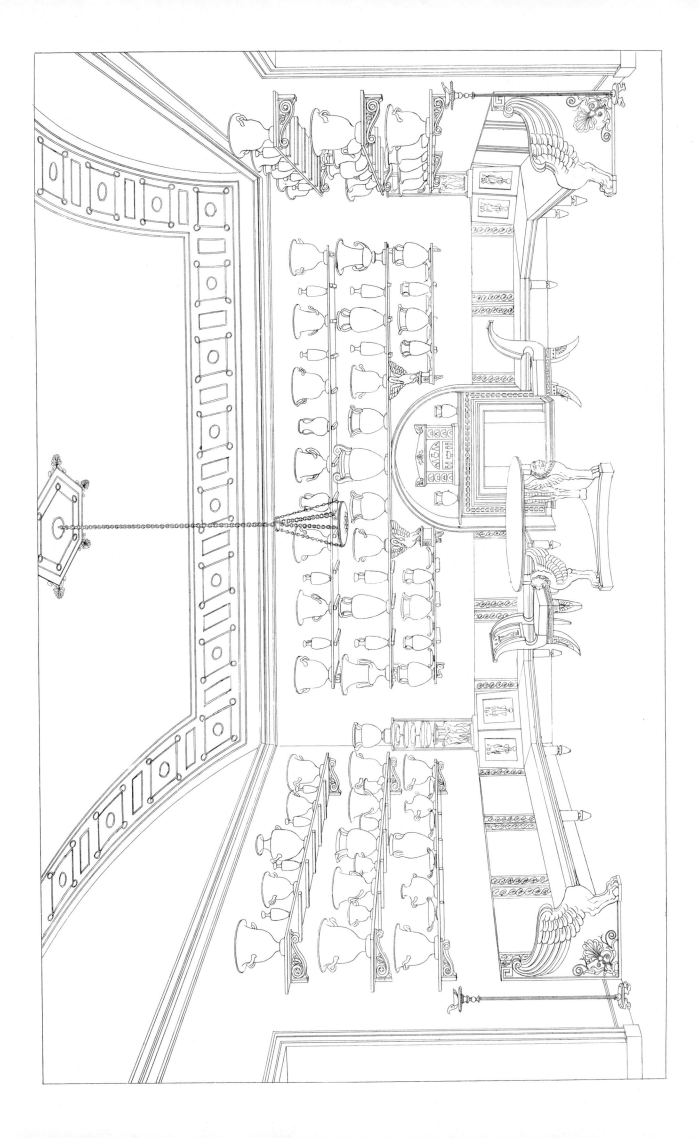

buildings in India, of Moorifh architecture. Some part of the arrangement and decoration of the room were, for this reafon, borrowed from the Saracenic ftyle; though, from the unavoidable intermixture of other productions of art, of a totally different character with the pictures aforementioned, it was impoffible to adhere to the Moorifh ftyle in the greater part of the detail.

A low fofa, after the eaftern fafhion, fills the corners of this room. Its ceiling, imitated from thofe prevailing in Turkifh palaces, confifts of a canopy of trellice-work, or reeds, tied together with ribbons. The border and the compartments of this ceiling difplay foliage, flowers, peacock's feathers, and other ornaments of a rich hue, and of a delicate texture, which, from the lightnefs of their weight, feem peculiarly adapted for this lofty and fufpended fituation. Perfian carpets cover the floor.

As the colours of this room, in compliance with the oriental tafte, are everywhere very vivid, and very ftrongly contrafted, due attention has been paid to their gradually lightening, as the eye rofe from the fkirting to the cornice. The tint of the fofa is deep crimfon; that of the walls fky blue; and that of the ceiling pale yellow, intermixed with azure and with fea green. Ornaments of gold, in various fhades, relieve and harmonize thefe colours. Round the room are placed incenfe urns, caffolettes, flower bafkets, and other vehicles of natural and artificial perfumes.

PLATE VII.

The central object in this room is a fine marble group, executed by Mr. Flaxman, and reprefenting Aurora vifiting Cephalus on mount Ida. The whole furrounding decoration has been rendered, in fome degree, analogous to thefe perfonages, and to the face of nature at the moment when the firft of the two, the goddefs of the morn, is fuppofed to announce approaching day. Round the bottom of the room ftill reign the emblems of night. In the rail of a black marble table are introduced medallions of the god of fleep and of the goddefs of night. The bird confecrated to the latter deity perches on the pillars of a black marble chimneypiece, whofe broad frieze is ftudded with golden ftars. The fides of the room difplay, in fatin curtains, draped in ample folds over pannels of looking-glafs, and edged with black velvet, the fiery hue which fringes the clouds juft before funrife: and in a ceiling of cooler fky blue are fown, amidft a few ftill unextinguifhed luminaries of the night, the rofes which the harbinger of day, in her courfe, fpreads on every fide around her.

The pedeftal of the group offers the torches, the garlands, the wreaths, and the other infignia belonging to the miftrefs of Cephalus, difpofed around the fatal dart of which fhe made her lover a prefent. The broad band which girds the top of the room, contains medallions of the ruddy goddefs and of

the Phrygian youth, intermixed with the inftruments and the emblems of the chace, his favourite amufement. Figures of the youthful hours, adorned with wreaths of foliage, adorn part of the furniture, which is chiefly gilt, in order to give more relief to the azure, the black, and the orange compartments of the hangings.

PLATE VIII.

Happening to poffefs feveral Egyptian antiquities, wrought in varioufly coloured materials, fuch as granite, ferpentine, porphyry, and bafalt, of which neither the hue nor the workmanfhip would have well accorded with thofe of my Greek ftatues, chiefly executed in white marble alone, I thought it beft to fegregate thefe former, and to place them in a feparate room, of which the decoration fhould, in its character, bear fome analogy to that of its contents. Accordingly, the ornaments that adorn the walls of this little canopus are, partly, taken from Egyptian fcrolls of papyrus; thofe that embellifh the ceiling, from Egyptian mummy cafes; and the prevailing colours of both, as well as of the furniture, are that pale yellow and that blueifh green which hold fo confpicuous a rank among the Egyptian pigments; here and there relieved by maffes of black and of gold.

Let me however avail myself of the defcription of this room, to urge young artifts never to adopt, except from motives more weighty than a mere aim at novelty, the Egyptian ftyle of ornament. The hieroglyphic figures, fo univerfally employed by the Egyptians, can afford us little pleafure on account of their meaning, fince this is feldom intelligible: they can afford us ftill lefs gratification on account of their outline, fince this is never agreeable; at leaft in as far as regards thofe fmaller details, which alone are fufceptible of being introduced in our confined fpaces. Real Egyptian monuments, built of the hardeft materials, cut out in the moft prodigious blocks, even where they pleafe not the eye, through the elegance of their fhapes, ftill amaze the intellect, through the immenfity of their fize, and the indeftructibility of their nature. Modern imitations of thofe wonders of antiquity, compofed of lath and of plafter, of callico and of paper, offer no one attribute of folidity or grandeur to compenfate for their want of elegance and grace, and can only excite ridicule and contempt.

PLATE IX.

Sideboard adorned with emblems of Bacchus and of Ceres. Cellaret ornamented with amphoræ and with figures, allufive to the liquid element. To the right, a floping altar

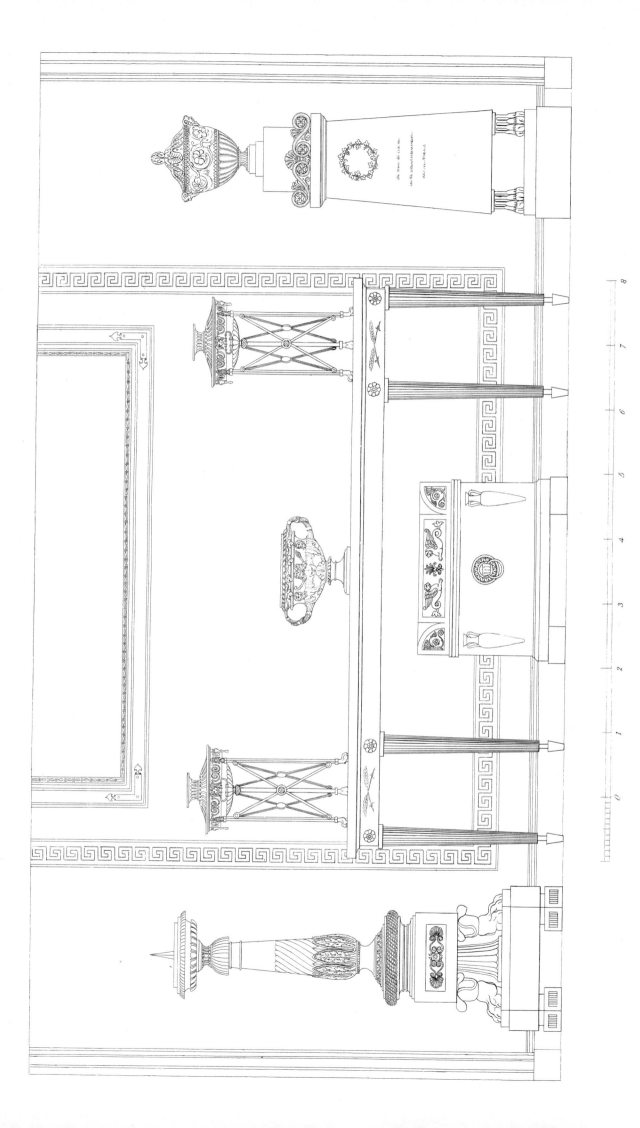

or pedeftal, furmounted by a vafe. To the left, a lofty candelabrum, deftined to fupport a torch. On the table, a vafe with Bacchanalian marks, placed between two caffolettes: over the fame a picture, reprefenting a Bacchanalian proceffion: the picture-frame of mahogany and gold, ftrengthened at the corners by metal gilt clafps.

PLATE X.

Clofet or boudoir fitted up for the reception of a few Egyptian, Hindoo, and Chinefe idols and curiofities. The fides of this Lararium are formed of pillars, and the top of laths, of bamboo. Over thefe hangs a cotton drapery, in the form of a tent. One end of this tabernacle is open, and difplays a mantle-piece in the fhape of an Egyptian portico, which, by being placed againft a back ground of looking-glafs, appears entirely infulated. On the fteps of this portico are placed idols, and in its furface are inferted bas-reliefs.

PLATE XI.

No. 1 and 2. Front and end of a large library or writing-table, flanked with paper preſſes, or eſcrutoirs. The tops that terminate theſe preſſes preſent the ſhape of ancient Greek houſe roofs. Their extremities or pediments contain the heads of the patron and patroneſs of ſcience, of Apollo and of Minerva.

No. 3 and 4. Front and ſide of an arm-chair.

No. 5. Flat cup of roſſo antico, placed on tripod of bronze: bronze ornaments round the triangular pedeſtal. For the plan of this pedeſtal ſee Plate 55, No. 3.

Many of the inſulated ornaments, which adorn the various objects of uſe and of decoration, in wood and ſtone, here re-preſented, are in bronze, left ſimply to exhibit its own green patina. Theſe ornaments in bronze, which, being caſt, may, wherever a frequent repetition of the ſame forms is required, be wrought at a much cheaper rate than ornaments in other materials, only producible through the more tedious proceſs of carving; which, moreover, may be indiſcriminately affixed to objects in wood, or ſtone, or metal, or porcelaine, or any other; which, thirdly, when once placed, ſeem liable to little or no injury or diſcolouring either from the effects of weather or wear, of carriage or dirt; which, in the fourth place, no-wiſe irretrievably cohering with the body of the object, on whoſe ſurface they are ſituated, may, either on a renewal or a change of habitation, be taken off things become uſeleſs or

decayed, however long they have adhered to the fame, and be applied to new objects; and which, finally, on a defire to increafe the richnefs of their appearance, may, however long they have ferved in their green and naked ftate, ftill affume a richer garb, be gilt and be burnifhed, feem, in a country where fuel is lefs expenfive than hands, and where the at-mofphere, charged with damp and with fmoke, is feldom pure, preferable to fculptured ornaments, whofe original fabrication, in any quantities, is more expenfive; whofe texture is more brittle; whofe hue is more delicate; which, eafily difcoloured, and eafily broken, are difficult to clean, and more difficult to mend; and which, laftly, never fufceptible of being fevered from the object to which they belong, muft follow its fate, and perifh with the fame.

PLATE XII.

No. 1 and 2.   End and front of a table.

No. 3, 4, and 5.   Different ftools.

No. 6 and 7.   End and front of a table.

1

2

3

4

5

7

6

PLATE XIII.

No. 1 and 2. End and front of a table, in the boudoir, or repofitory of Egyptian, Hindoo, and other curiofities.

No. 3. Front of a table, in the room dedicated to Aurora. Females, emblematic of the four horæ or parts of the day, fupport its rail, the frieze of which contains medallions of the deities of night and fleep. On the table ftands a clock, carried by a figure of Ifis, or the moon, adorned with her crefcent.

PLATE XIV.

No. 1. Fire fcreen. A profile of the fame fcreen may be feen in Plate 51, No. 3.

No. 2. Pedeftal, belonging to the group of Aurora and Cephalus, and adorned with ornaments, emblematic of thefe perfonages; fuch as torches, flowers, a dart, a diadem of ftars, and the head of Jupiter Serapis or Pluto, figurative of death.

No. 3 and 4. Front and profile of a dreffing-glafs.

1
2
3
4

PLATE XV.

No. 1. Tripod table, fupported by chimæras. A plan of this table is found in Plate 55, No. 1.

No. 2. End of a table, belonging to the mufic room, and adorned with an antique lyre.

No. 3. Table, on which ftands a glazed cafe or fhade, between two candlefticks.

No. 4 and 5. Front and end of a table, under which is introduced a flower bafket.

1

2

3

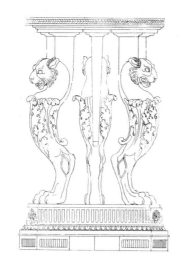

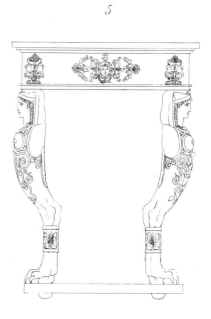

4

5

PLATE XVI.

No. 1.   Chimney-piece in black marble, belonging to the Aurora room, and decorated with emblems of night in gilt bronze.

No. 2.   Table, belonging to the Egyptian room.   On this table ftands, between two Egyptian ædiculæ, containing idols, and fupporting Canopufes, a cup of bafalt.   Under the table lies a lion of the fame material.

1

2

PLATE XVII.

No. 1 and 2. Front and end of a glazed cafe, containing a fmall mummy, and of the floping or pyramidic pedeftal which fupports this cafe. Within this pedeftal, which is perforated, ftands an antique cinerary urn of Egyptian or oriental alabafter. Two feated figures of priefts, wearing mafks of various animals, guard the entrance: over which hovers a winged Ifis, emblematic of the immortality of the foul.

No. 3 and 4. Front and end of fettees, belonging to the Egyptian room.

No. 5. Bronze tripod, with hinges and fliders, made to take to pieces and to fold up, after the manner of ancient tripods.

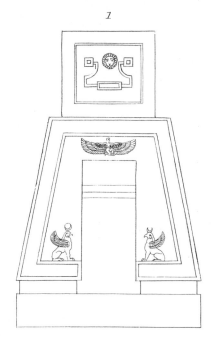

1

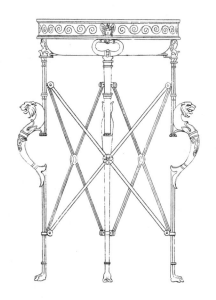

5

2

3

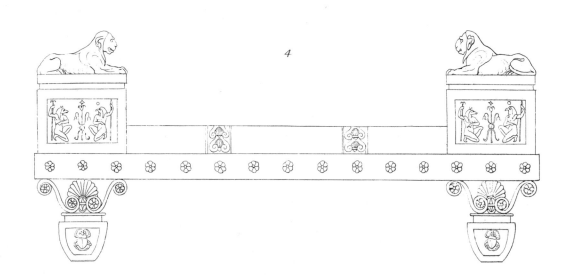

4

PLATE XVIII.

No. 1.   Mantle-piece: the bas reliefs on the jambs reprefent candelabra, furmounted by pine cones, like thofe ufed in Italy to light fires.

No. 2.   Pole fire fcreen, in the fhape of a Roman fhield, adorned with Jove's fulmen, as wrought by the Cyclops.

"........Tris imbris torti radios, tris nubis aquofæ,

" Addiderant; rutili tris ignis, et alitis auftri."

ÆN. lib. 8.

No. 3 and 4.   Front and fide view of a deep arm-chair, adorned with a chimæra, copied from a farcophagus in the collection of Prince Brafchi at Rome.

The correfponding chair is adorned with a griffin, copied from the fame farcophagus.

No. 5.   Settee belonging to the Lararium. Its frieze contains, in fmall, the figures of the twelve great gods of the Greeks and Romans, as reprefented in the old ftiff ftyle of workmanfhip, round the Bocca di pozzo, in the Capitol.

PLATE XIX.

No. 1.   Tripod table.

No. 2.   Settee.

No. 3 and 4.   Chairs.

No. 5.   Round table.

No. 6 and 7.   Front and fide view of ftone feats, adorned with fphinxes and Lotus flowers.

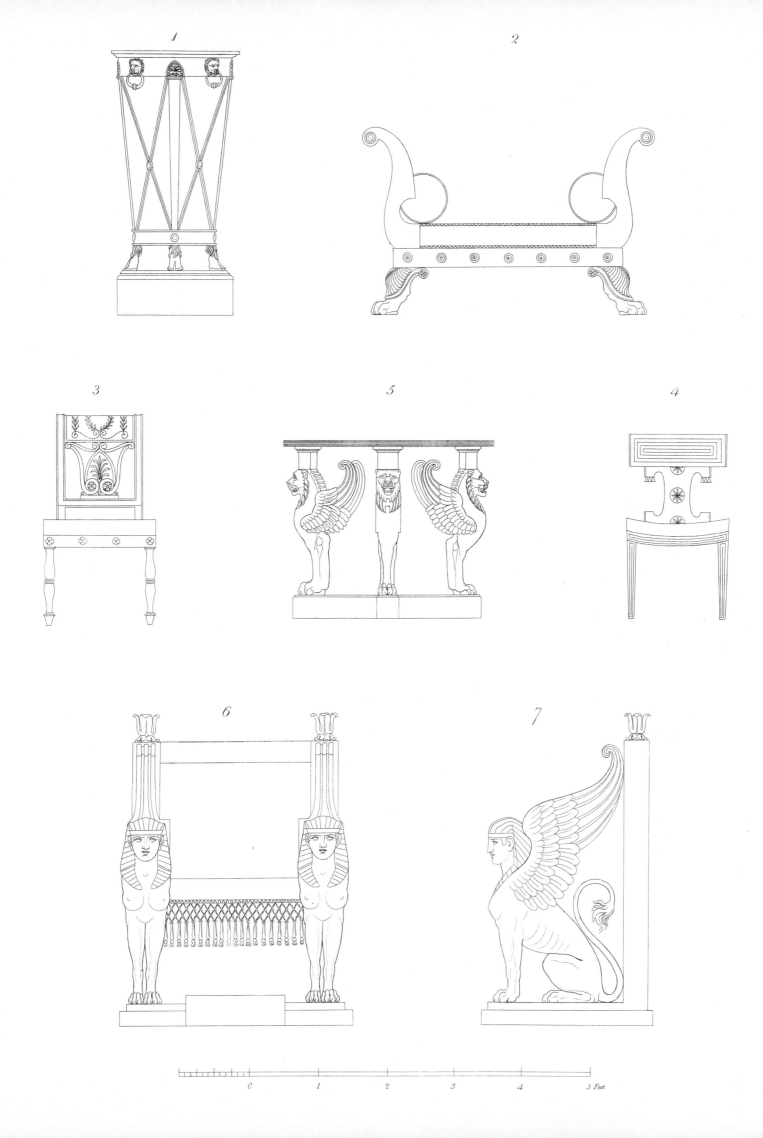

1

2

3

5

4

6

7

0   1   2   3   4   5 Feet

PLATE XX.

No. 1. Side of a table.

No. 2. End of the fame table.

No. 3 and 4. Front and fide of an arm-chair, after the manner of the ancient curule chairs.

No. 5 and 6. Front and fide of an arm-chair.

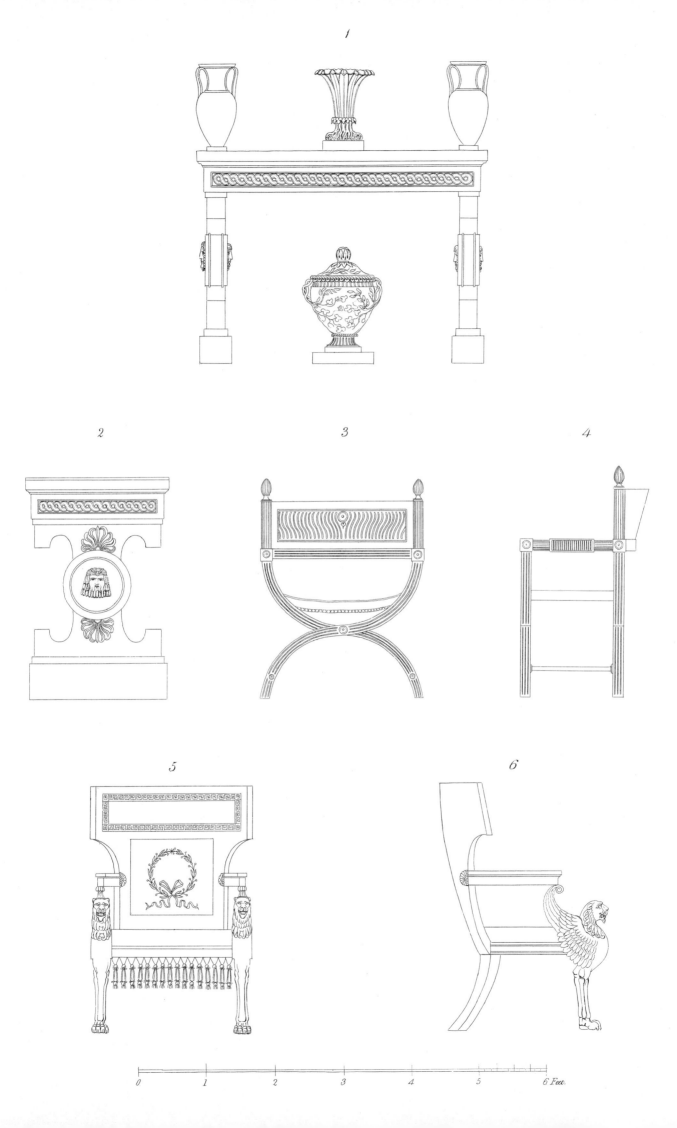

1

2   3   4

5   6

0   1   2   3   4   5   6 Feet.

PLATE XXI.

Stand of bronze and gold, fupporting a large fea-green China bowl, adorned with the meander and the Lotus flower. The ornaments of this ftand, fuch as the Iris, the water-leaf, and the fwans, are chiefly borrowed from the aquatic reign.

PLATE XXII.

No. 1 and 2. Two views of a tea-table, with very projecting horizontal handles. Under this tea-table, on a tablet fupported by pheafant's feet, ending in a fcroll, ftands a tea-cheft with perpendicular handles.

No. 3. Tripod table.

No. 4. Bronze candelabrum.

No. 5 and 6. Front and fide of a large arm-chair.

_1_

_2_

_3_

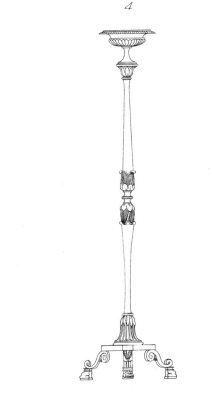

_4_

_5_

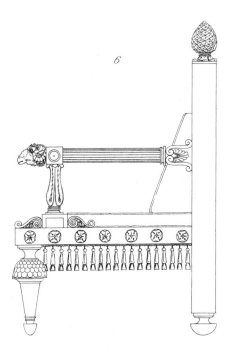

_6_

0   1   2   3   4 Feet

PLATE XXIII.

Upright piano-forte. Two genii, contending for a wreath form a group round the key-hole.

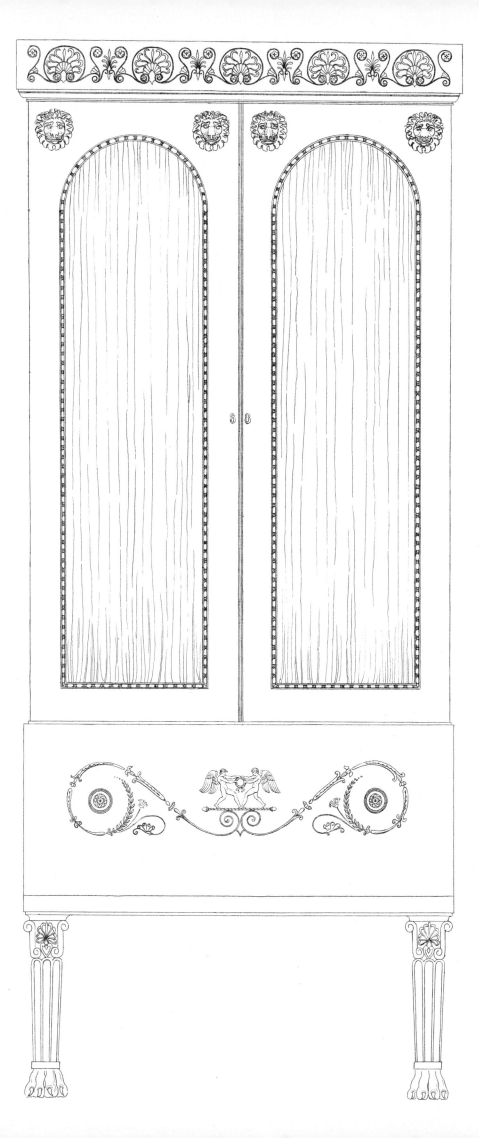

PLATE XXIV.

No. 1. End of a narrow pier table, from the rail of which hangs a broad fringe, carved in wood.

No. 2 and 3. Mahogany chairs, inlaid in metal and ebony.

Thefe fpecies of inlayings in metal, on a ground of ebony or dyed wood, feem peculiarly adapted to the nature of the mahogany furniture fo much in ufe in this country, which they enliven, without preventing it, by any raifed ornaments, from being conftantly rubbed, and kept free from duft and dirt. At Paris they have been carried to a great degree of elegance and perfection. The metal ornament, and the ground of ftained wood in which it is inferted, being, there, ftamped together, and cut out, through dint of the fame fingle mechanical procefs, they are always fure of fitting each other to the greateft degree of nicety.

See Plate 26, No. 6, a fide view of the chair, No. 2.

No. 4. Wine cooler, in the fhape of an antique bath or lavacrum.

No. 5. Candelabrum, compofed of a Lotus flower iffuing from a bunch of oftrich feathers.

No. 6. Pedeftals belonging to a fideboard; imitated from an Etrufcan altar in the villa Borghefe.

For the plan of this pedeftal fee Plate 55, No. 2.

PLATE XXV.

No. 1.   Stool.

No. 2.   Tripod table.   For the plan of this table fee Plate 55, No. 5.

No. 3.   Mantle-piece of white marble, ftudded with bronze ornaments.   The candelabrum placed between two Mythriac figures, and the heads of Vefta and of Vulcan are emblematic of the worfhip of fire.

No. 4.   Side view of a chair.

No. 5.   Little round monopodium or ftand, of which the top, through means of a flider and a fcrew, is capable of being raifed or lowered at pleafure.

1

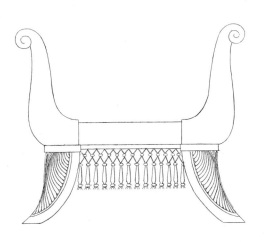

2

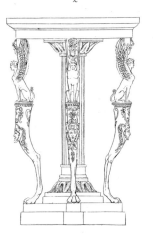

3

4

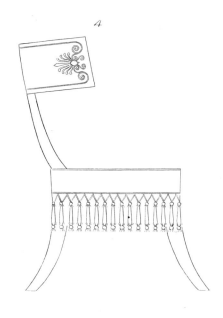

5

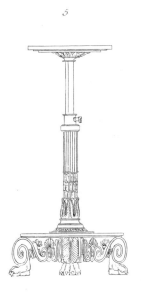

PLATE XXVI.

No. 1 and 2. Two chairs.

No. 3. Front view of a table, on which ſtands a vaſe, between two tripods.

No. 4. Box or coffer, imitated from an ancient ſarcophagus of verde antico, at preſent ſerving as a fountain of ablution in the ſmall moſque, called Kliſſie Dgiamee, at Conſtantinople.

No. 5 and 6. Side views of two mahogany chairs. No. 5 is the ſide view of the chair, Plate 24, No. 3.

No. 7. End of a table.

No. 8 and 9. Settee. The ends are copied from a fine antique chimæra of marble, in the ſtudio of Cavaceppi at Rome.

3

1

2

4

5

7

6

8

9

0   1   2   3   4   5

PLATE XXVII.

No. 1. Receffes in the fhape of ancient hypogea, or niches for cinerary urns, deftined for the reception of fmall fepulchral vafes.

No. 2. Frame, containing a picture in enamel, reprefenting a fleeping Venus, furrounded by Cupids. The top or pediment of this frame is adorned with medallions of the goddefs and of Mars. Its jambs or pilafters are ornamented with figures of dancing nymphs, holding up wreaths of myrtle.

1

2

0   1

PLATE XXVIII.

No. 1.   Candelabrum deftined to carry a torch.

No. 2 and 3.   Side and end of a couch: a greyhound lies watching on the footboard, after the manner of fimilar animals on Gothic farcophagi.

No. 4 and 5.   Front and profile of a fire fcreen, with wings to draw out.

No. 6 and 7.   Side and end of a couch, fhaped like the ancient Triclinia: a leopard's fkin thrown over the feat.

PLATE XXIX.

No. 1. Folding ftool, with ram's head and hoof extremities: loofe drapery thrown over the feat.

No. 2. Folding ftool, formed of antique fwords, croffed.

No. 3. Bedftead of mahogany and bronze. The pilafters ornamented with figures of Night, rifing on her crefcent, and fpreading her poppies.

No. 4. Toilet ftand for ewer and bafon. Sea monfters and other aquatic emblems round the frieze.

No. 5. End of the fofa in the room, Plate 5.

PLATE XXX.

Chandelier of bronze and gold; ornamented with a crown of ſtars over a wreath of night-ſhade.

0   1   2   3 Feet

PLATE XXXI.

Old China jar, of a rich purple hue, mounted in or-moulu.

PLATE XXXII.

No. 1.   Tripod table, in mahogany and gold.

No. 2.   Plan of the fame.

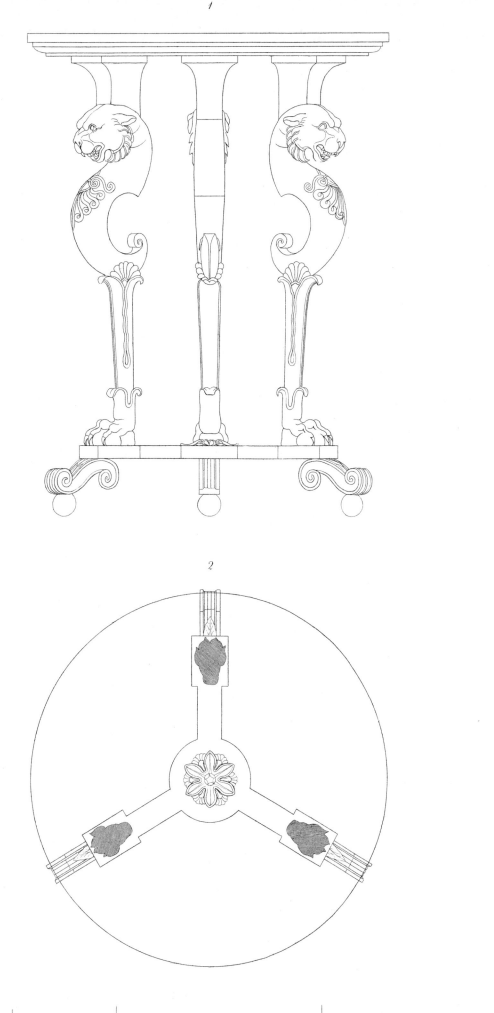

1

2

2 Feet

PLATE XXXIII.

Dreffing-table, in mahogany and gold, fupported by heads and claws of Sphinxes: vafe of alabafter placed on the table.

PLATE XXXIV.

Vaſe of bronze and gold: ſhape and handles copied from a Greek vaſe of white marble in the muſeum at Portici. A group of Apollo Citharædus, and Genius, borrowed from a bas-relief in the Britiſh Muſeum, together with other emblems of Apollo, ornament this vaſe.

PLATE XXXV.

Vafe of bronze and gold, of the fame fhape as the former, and intended as a companion to the fame, but ornamented with Bacchanalian mafks, vine wreaths, and other emblems of Bacchus.

PLATE XXXVI.

Side view of the vafe, Plate 35.

PLATE XXXVII.

Comic and tragic maſks, of Silenus, of Bacchante, of Juno, and of Hercules, taken from antique ornaments.

PLATE XXXVIII.

No. 1.   Bottom of bronze lamp, in the room, Plate 5.

No. 2 and 3.   Mofaic borders of floor and ceiling.

2

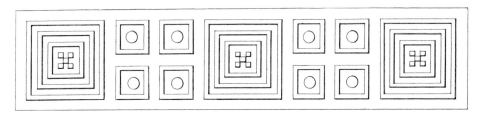

1

3

PLATE XXXIX.

Top and elevation of a round monopodium or table in
mahogany, inlaid in ebony and filver.

1

2

1   2   3   4   5   6 *Feet.*

PLATE XL.

No. 1. Vafe of alabafter.

No. 2 and 3. Side and front of a ftool; the elbows formed by fwans, on a plinth ornamented with the Grecian fcroll, emblematic of waves.

No. 4. Dreffing-table, fupported by female terms, copied from the Inftitute at Bologna.

No. 5. Picture frame.

No. 6. Side view of a chair.

1

2

4

3

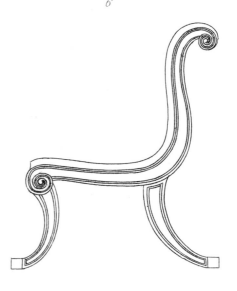

5

6

PLATE XLI.

No. 1. Ornament of the corner tiles on the pediment of the library table, Plate 11, No. 1.

No. 2. Ornament of the femi-circular tiles on the roof or top of the library table, Plate 11, No. 2.

No. 3. Ornament of the corner tiles on the pediment of the dreffing-glafs, Plate 14, No. 3.

No. 4. End of the clafps of the tea-cheft, under the tea-table, Plate 22, No. 2.

No. 5. Chain belonging to the bronze lamp, in the room Plate 5.

No. 6. Top of the legs which fupport the caffolettes on the fideboard, Plate 9.

No. 7. Capital of the pilafters belonging to the dreffing-glafs, Plate 14, No. 3.

No. 8. Rofette, on the cover of the bronze and gold vafes, Plates 34, 35, and 36.

No. 9. Capital of the pilafters belonging to the fettee, Plate 26, No. 8 and 9.

No. 10. Ancient drinking-horn.

No. 11. Ornament formed of a fwan carrying a mafk; introduced in the caffolettes on the fideboard, Plate 9.

No. 12. Claw fupporting a plinth.

No. 13. Ornament in the frieze of the table, Plate 15, No. 4.

No. 14. Ornament in the frieze of the library table, Plate 11, No. 2.

No. 15. Other ornament in ditto.

PLATE XLII.

Elevation and plan of a bronze gilt chandelier, ornamented with drops, prifms, &c. of cut glafs.

1

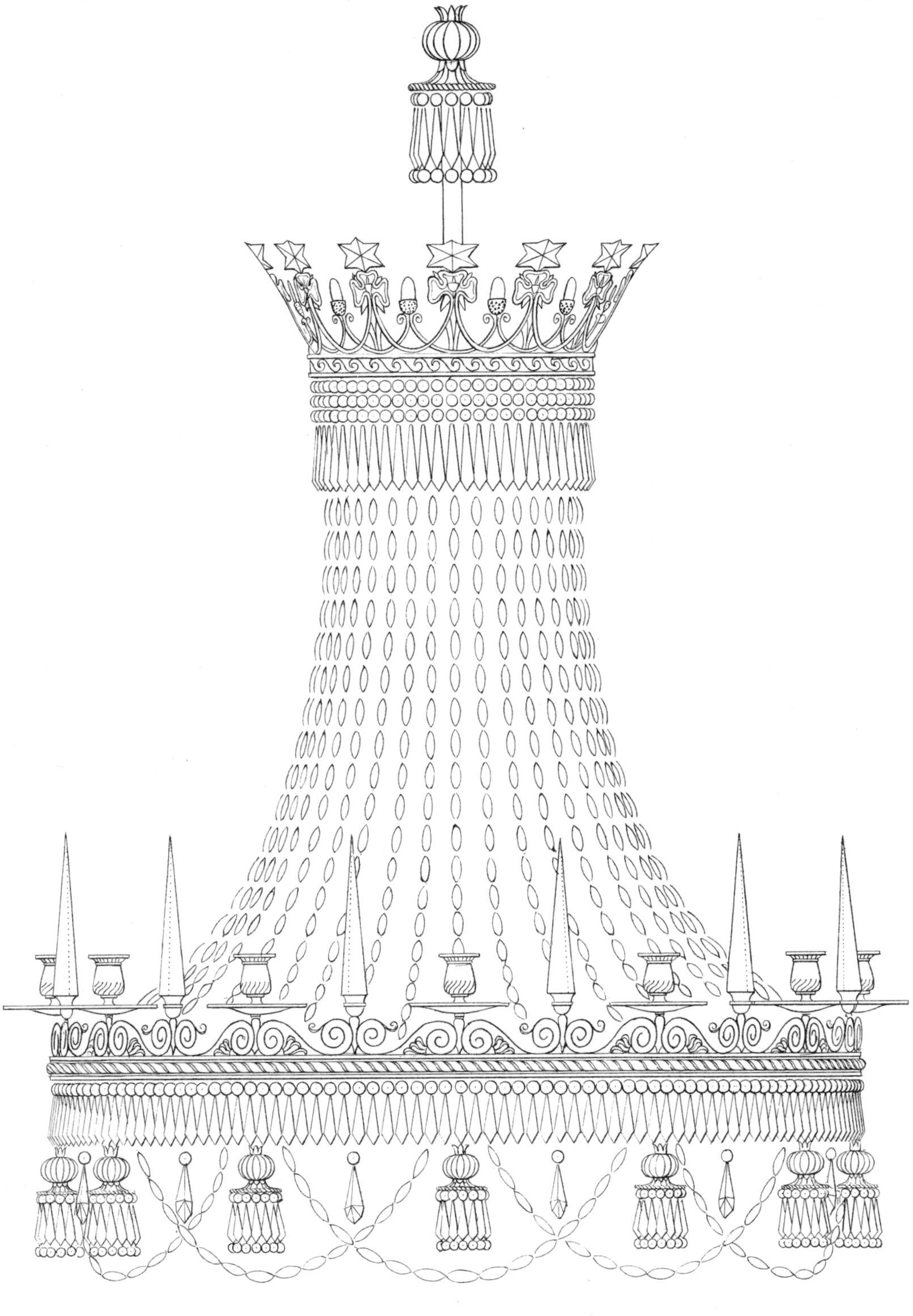

2

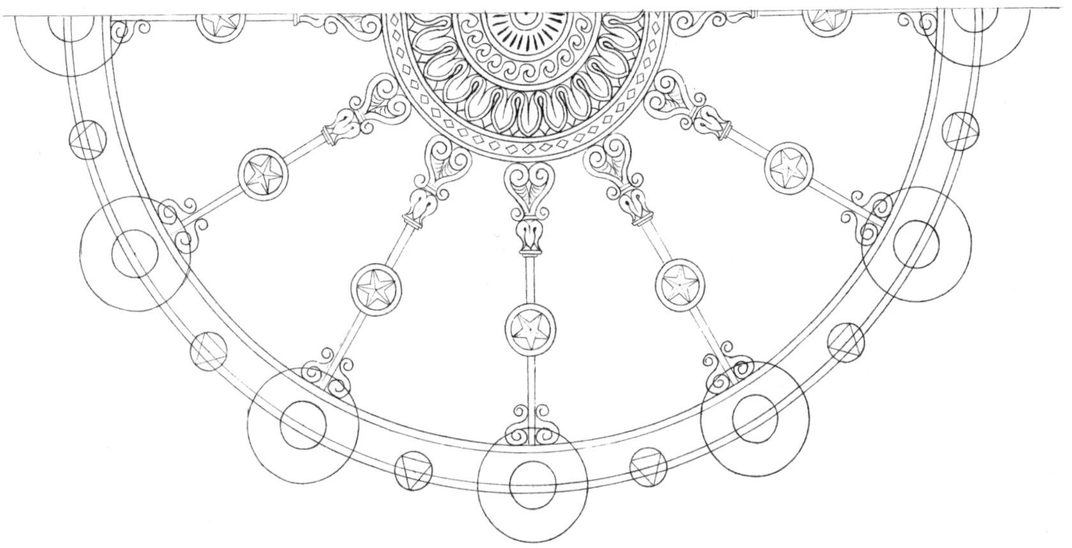

PLATE XLIII.

No. 1.   Sconce or girandole for four lights, in bronze and gold.

No. 2.   Profile of ditto.

No. 3.   Other fconce or girandole for four lights.

The artificial lights, which our habitations require at night, in order to render the furrounding objects vifible, cannot be prevented from themfelves, in fome meafure, becoming the predominant vifible object. Hence the greateft attention fhould be adhibited to place, not only the different groups, but the different lights compofing each group, in fuch exact fym-metry with regard to each other, as may prevent their pre-fenting, in any point of view, an indiftinct and confufed glare. Cluftered and often zig-zagged as are the branches of the girandoles, in moft of our public places and private rooms, the lights which they carry not only diffufe lefs general fplen-dour, but look individually lefs diftinct and lefs grand, than if they were made to range on long horizontal lines, at equal diftances from each other.

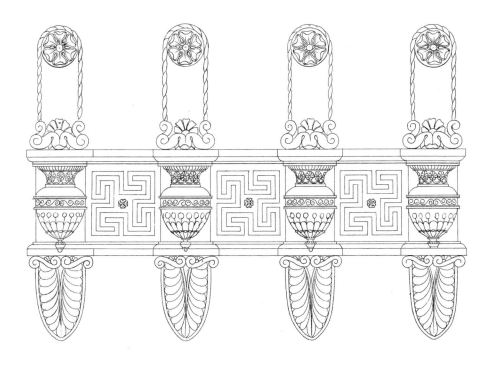

1

2

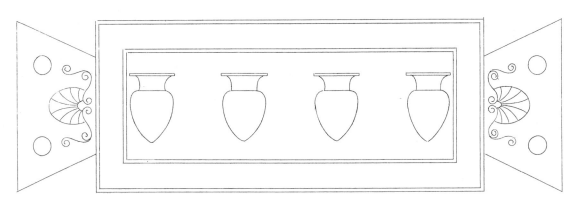

3

1 2 3 4 5 6 7 8 9 10 11

0

PLATE XLIV.

End view of a cradle in mahogany, ornamented in gilt bronze, with emblems of night, of fleep, of dreams, and of hope.

PLATE XLV.

Elevation of a folding door, fhewing different ways in which the compartments or pannels may be ornamented.

At Florence I was much ftruck with the grandeur which the doors of the Ufficii, and of other public buildings, derived from the equal divifion of their compartments, and from the number of large brafs nail-heads with which the intervals between thefe compartments were ftudded round. At Rome alfo I was much pleafed with the magnificent fimplicity which the door-ways of moft handfome apartments prefented, in confequence of their frames being a fimple flat and broad band, either compofed of, or reprefenting fome rich marble. This fafhion might, I conceive, be imitated in this country, where the leaves of doors, in mahogany, ftudded with gilt nails, and their frames, in fcagliola, would have a peculiarly rich and beautiful effect.

PLATE XLVI.

No. 1. Mantle-piece of black marble, copied from the facade of a fepulchral chamber, hewn in the folid body of a perpendicular rock, on the coaft of ancient Lycia, and on the fpot where formerly ftood the city of Anti-phellos, mentioned by Strabo. It reprefents a facade or fcreen of rude and maffy timber-work, in which may be difcerned the upright pofts, the tranfverfe beams, the rafters, the wedges, and the bolts.

This mantle-piece is in the Egyptian room, Plate 8. The ornaments on its fhelf and on its fender have been copied from Egyptian idols and bas-reliefs, partly exifting in the Capitol and in the Vatican, and partly reprefented in the plates of the Herculaneum collection and of Denon's work.

No. 2 and 3. Front and fide view of a large arm-chair, in the Egyptian room, Plate 8. The crouching priefts fupporting the elbows are copied from an Egyptian idol in the Vatican: the winged Ifis placed in the rail is borrowed from an Egyptian mummy-cafe in the Inftitute at Bologna: the Canopufes are imitated from the one in the Capitol; and the other ornaments are taken from various monuments at Thebes, Tentyris, &c.

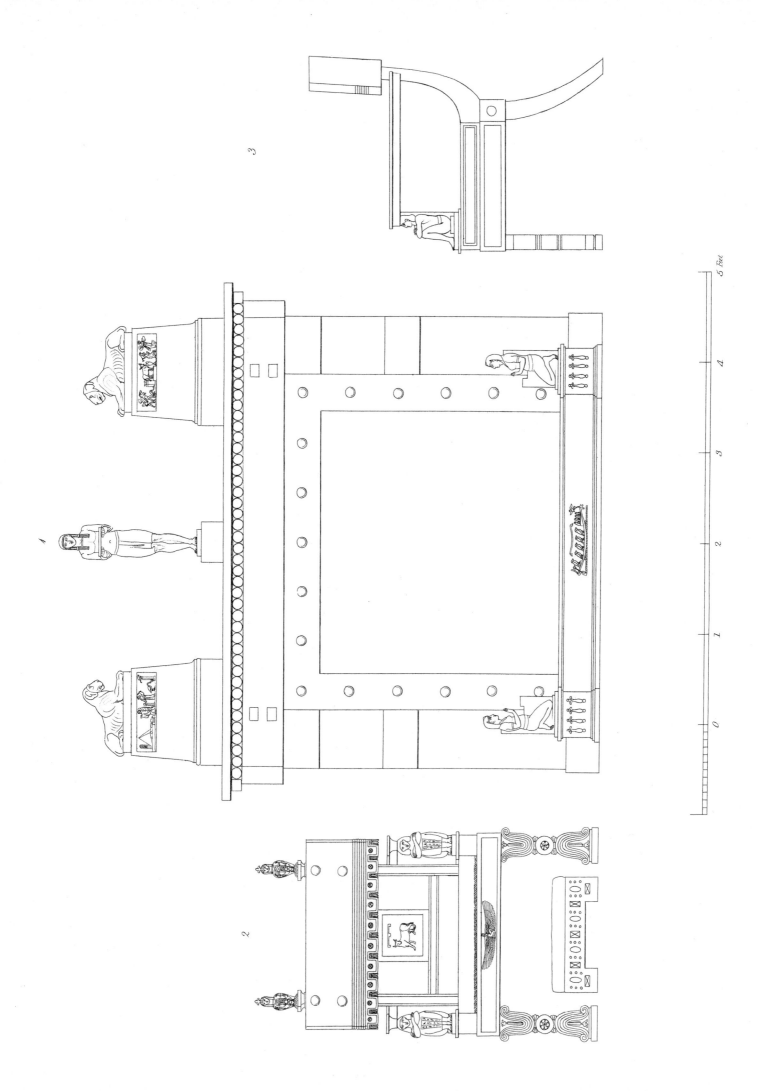

5 Feet

1

2

3

PLATE XLVII.

Group, compofed of various utenfils, fuch as a cup, a vafe, an ewer, a cafferole, an ice pail, a ragout difh, and a fugar bafon, executed partly in filver and partly in bronze.

The wide and flat bottom, exhibited by the ice pail here reprefented, is prefumed to offer a fhape more appropriate to the purpofes of that fpecies of veffel, than the long neck or ftalk, and the contracted bottom, difplayed by the generality of ice pails ufed in England, which are nothing more than imitations of a tall and flender flower pot. This more capacious and more fteady form offers at once more room for ice round the bottom of the decanter, is lefs liable to the danger of being upfet, and raifes the decanter lefs above the level of the arm.

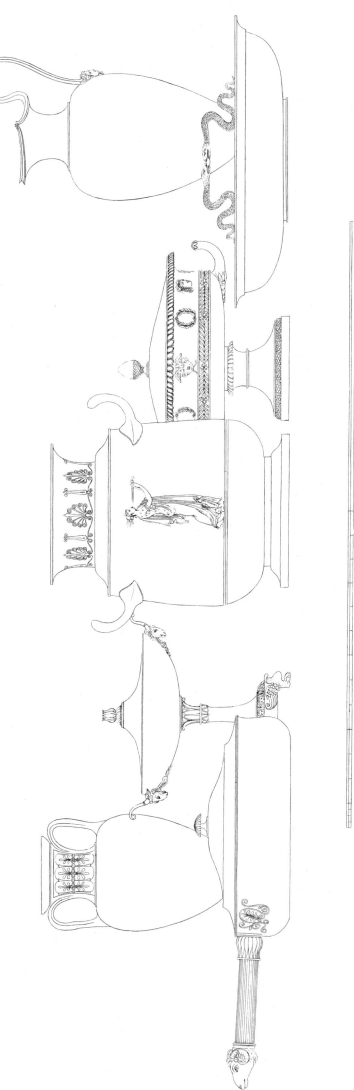

PLATE XLVIII.

No. 1.   Mantle-piece, with various ornaments.

No. 2 and 3.   Vaſes and cippuſes of different marbles, copied from antiques in the Albani and Barbarini collections.

PLATE XLIX.

Group, compofed of various utenfils in filver and in bronze; namely, a vafe, a tea urn, an ewer, a candleftick, and a cafket.

PLATE L.

No. 1. Mantle-piece, belonging to the eating-room, to which belongs the fideboard reprefented Plate 9.

The flab or fhelf of this mantle-piece is very wide and projecting; and the ftiles or jambs are made to flope downwards, in the manner of brackets; as may be feen in the profile of the mantle-piece, given in the next plate. Over the mantle-piece project two antique horfes heads, in allufion to the name of Φιλιππος, infcribed on the buft placed between them. Bacchanalian mafks adorn the jambs.

No. 2 and 3. Candelabra, or ftands: the one furmounted by an ewer, the other by a flower bafket, in gilt bronze.

I avail myfelf of the occafion of the buft reprefented in this plate, to notice an error of tafte, into which have fallen fome Englifh fculptors: no doubt in imitation of the French fculptors of the laft century; fince the practice which I allude to feems fanctioned by no ancient example whatever, of a pure ftyle of art. I mean the fafhion of reprefenting, in a buft, the head, not looking ftrait forward, and in the fame direction with the cheft, but turned over the fhoulder, and looking fideways: a pofition which, except in the bufts of Caracalla, no longer belonging to the pure ftyle of ancient art, is, I believe, found in no ancient bufts, that did not originally form part of entire ftatues, and are only preferved as fragments of fuch.

2

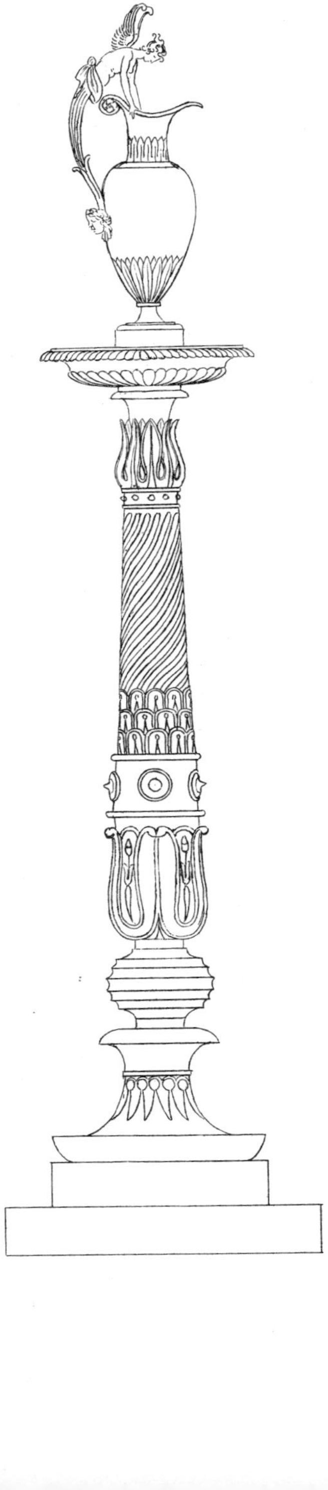

1

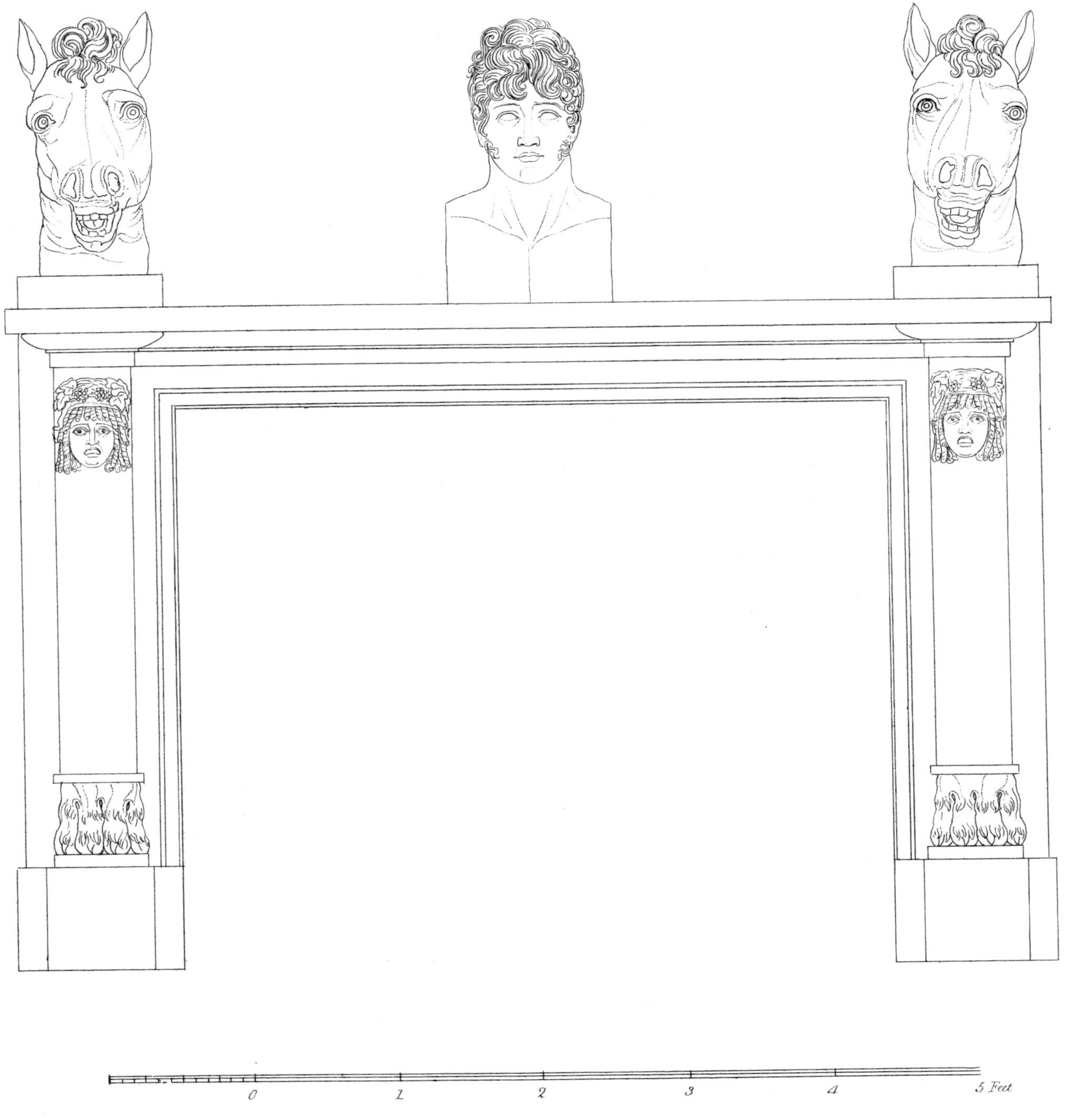

3

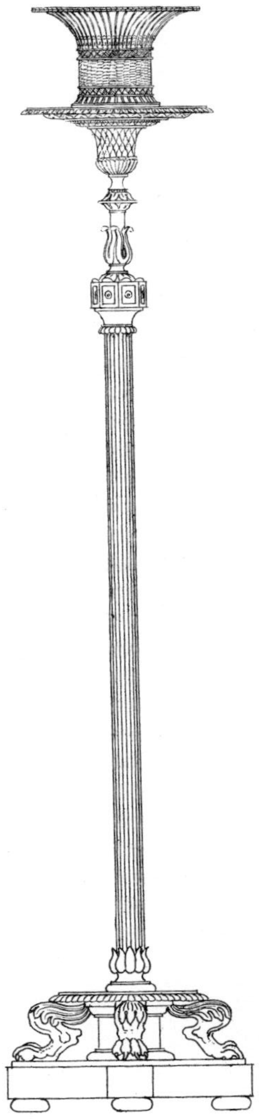

In a production of the pencil, which can only exhibit a face in a fingle afpect, if the moft ftriking or moft favourable view of that face be not a direct front view, there may, in the eligibility of bringing the features more in profile, be a very good reafon for turning the head fomewhat over the fhoulder. Nay, even in a work of the chiffel, if it be an entire ftatue, the peculiar attitude or action of the body may prefent a fufficient motive for giving fuch a turn to the head. But if a mere buft, which we may eafily view in every poffible afpect, by ourfelves moving round it, in place of being allowed to leave this tafk entirely to the beholder, be made itfelf to turn its face away from our fight, though it have not a body, to account for this lefs eafy and lefs ufual pofition of the head, the portrait lofes all claim to naturalnefs and truth; it forfeits the appearance of dignified fimplicity, which is fo effential and fo fafcinating, for an air of inane and pompous affectation; and it moreover, from the different direction given to the face and to the cheft, can feldom be fo fituated as not to look ill placed and awkward.

I fhall beg to add that the Grecian method of cutting the cheft fquare, and placing its whole mafs immediately on a term or other folid fupport, feems much preferable to the more prevailing Roman fafhion of rounding off that cheft, and balancing its center only on a flender and tottering pivot.

PLATE LI.

No. 1. Profile of the mantle-piece in the foregoing plate.

No. 2. End of a fettee, ornamented with the buft and emblems of Mercury; his caduceus and tortoife.

No. 3. Profile of the fire fcreen, Plate 14, No. 1.

PLATE LII.

Group compoſed of various utenſils in gold, in ſilver, and in ivory: a tea urn, a fruit baſket, an ewer, a candleſtick, a ſugar baſon, and a cup, ſurrounded by Nereids and Tritons.

The tea urn is the ſame of Plate 49, ſeen ſideways.

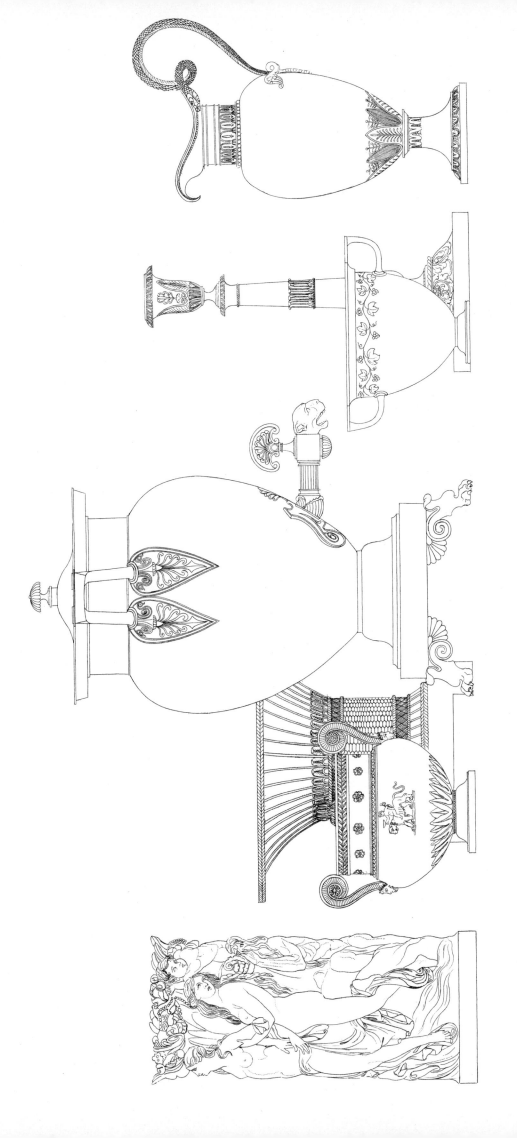

PLATE LIII.

No. 1. Profile of the Turkiſh picture frame reprefented in the title-page.

No. 2. Silk taffel.

No. 3. Griffins of the chandelier, Plate 30.

No. 4. Leg of the ſofa in the drawing-room, Plate 6.

No. 5. Profile of the picture frame, Plate 40, No. 5.

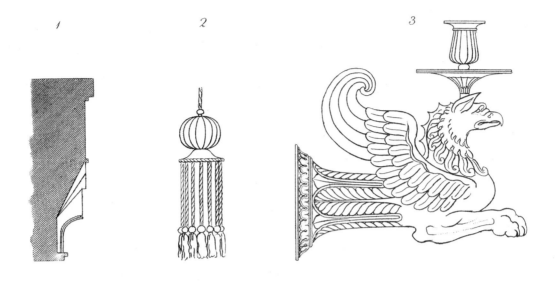

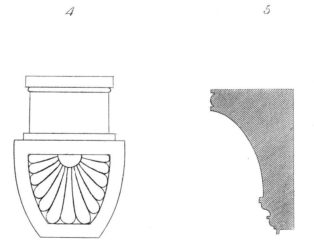

PLATE LIV.

No. 1 and 2. End and front of a fmall dreffing or toilet table, ornamented with the bird of Venus.

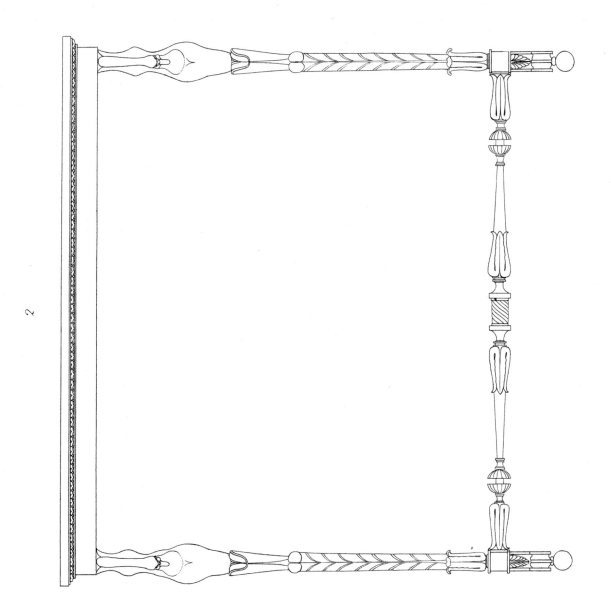

PLATE LV.

No. 1. Plan of the tripod, Plate 15, No. 1.

No. 2. Plan of the fideboard pedeftal, Plate 24, No. 6.

No. 3. Plan of the tripod, Plate 11, No. 5.

No. 4. Plan of the candelabrum, Plate 24, No. 5.

No. 5. Plan of the tripod table, Plate 25, No. 2.

No. 6. Plan of the monopodium or ftand, Plate 25, No. 5.

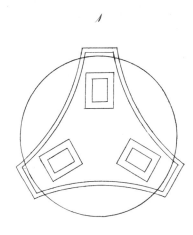

1

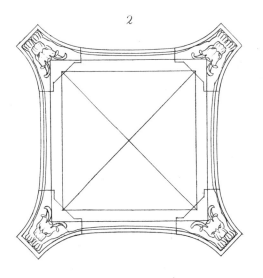

2

3

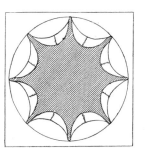

4

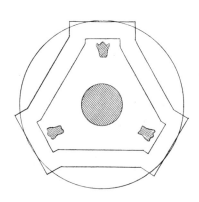

5

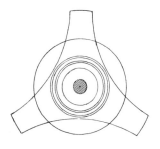

6

PLATE LVI.

Three lyres, imitated from the antique: the third is taken from a very fine fragment of a Greek fictile vafe, in my pof-feffion.

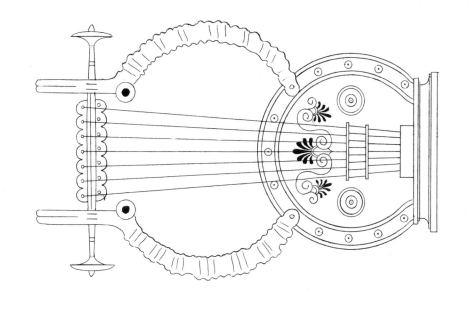

PLATE LVII.

Different heads of the Indian or bearded Bacchus. Grecian mythologifts tell us that Bacchus, the firft legiflator who attempted to civilize the Greeks, on his return from that region, which the Grecian philofophers venerated as the cradle of fcience and the earlieft feat of wifdom, namely, India, though ftill in the prime of youth, affected the gravity of old age, and let his beard grow, in order the more to refemble the Gymnofophifts, or fages of India, with whom he had converfed. In conformity with this fable, the Indian Bacchus or the legiflator, was ufually reprefented, not only with a long beard, but with the long hair hanging down the back, which was in the remoteft ages univerfally worn by the Greeks, and which, of all the goddeffes of Olympus, the ftarched and ftately Minerva alone ever continued, even in later times, uniformly to difplay, in defiance of more modern fafhions.

This long hair, both of the beard and of the head, ufed, in thofe early ages, to be twifted, by means of hot curling-irons, into the moft formal cork-fcrew ringlets, or fnail-fhell curls; in order to make it correfpond with the equally formal parallel or zig-zag folds, in which were difpofed, and no doubt were fixed by means of ftarching and of ironing, the folds of the drapery; and fuch is in fact the coftume ge-

nerally difplayed in the head-drefs and attire of the Indian Bacchus.

This head ufed frequently to be placed, by the ancients, on their cippufes or terms, and, from the formal fymmetry of its decorations, unites moft happily with architectural ornaments. I thought it a peculiarly appropriate termination to the pilafters of a prefs, containing a collection of thofe Greek fictile vafes, which were chiefly confecrated to the worfhip and allufive to the myfteries of Bacchus; and among the infinite variety of head-dreffes, which this head difplays in different ancient monuments, I chofe thofe here reprefented, as offering the moft ftriking, and, at the fame time, moft pleafing peculiarities.

PLATE LVIII.

Mantle-piece with femicircular opening.

PLATE LIX.

No. 1 and 2.   Arm-chairs.

No. 3.   Small ftand for a candleftick or vafe.

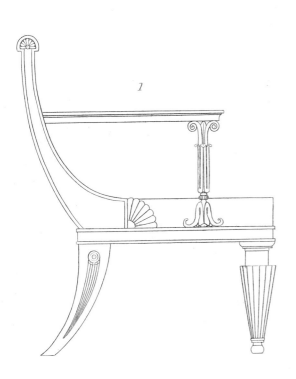

1

2

3

PLATE LX.

Trophy of Grecian armour; applicable to the cornice of a window curtain.

The explanation of the Plates terminating here, I ſhall conclude by ſubjoining a liſt of the different works, either repreſenting actual remains of antiquity, or modern compoſitions in the antique ſtyle, which have been of moſt uſe to me in my attempt to animate the different pieces of furniture here deſcribed, and to give each a peculiar countenance and character, a pleaſing outline, and an appropriate meaning. Theſe works are,

Stuart's Athens.

Le Roy's Monumens de la Grece.

Chandler's Ionia.

Pococke's Defcription of the Eaft.

Wood's Palmyra.

Wood's Balbec.

Norden's Egypt.

Denon's Egypt.

Daniell's Indian views.

Pitture, Statue, Bronzi, &c. di Ercolaneo.

Howel's Sicily.

Wood's Peftum.

Adams's Ruins of Spalatro.

Cleriffeau's Antiquités de la France.

Mofaiques d'Italica par Laborde.

Bellori's Picturæ Antiquæ.

Winckelman's Monumenti Antichi inediti.

Guattani's Monumenti inediti di Roma.

Vifconti's Mufeo Pio-Clementino.

Mufeo Capitolino.

Mufeum Florentinum.

Statue Antiche di San-Marco.

Montfaucon's Antiquities.

Caylus's Antiquities.

The Augufteum, or collection of antiquities in the Electoral gallery at Drefden.

Piranefi's works in general; and particularly his vafes, candelabra, and chimney-pieces.

D'Hancarville's Greek vafes.

Paſſeri's ditto.

Tifchbein's ditto; and the various other collections of paintings on Greek fictile vafes, formerly erroneoufly denominated Etrufcan, which afford the moft authentic and moft elegant fpecimens which we poſſefs, of Grecian rites, ceremonies, cuftoms, utenfils, and dreſſes.

Durand's Paralelle d'Edifices anciens et modernes: in which moft of the fine fpecimens of ancient ornamental architecture (though not reprefented, either with the greateft minutenefs or the greateft accuracy) are brought together in fo fmall a compafs as to render the work very ufeful to architects.

Percier's Edifices de Rome moderne.

Didot's folio Horace, with vignettes by Percier; fome of which offer exquifite reprefentations of the mode in which the ancient Romans ufed to decorate their town and country houfes.

Les Annales du Mufée Francais, par Landon.

Le Mufée des Monumens Francais, par Lenoir.

And laftly, Mr. Flaxman's compofitions from Efchylus and from Homer; which offer the fineft modern imitations I know of the elegance and beauty of the ancient Greek attire and furniture, armour and utenfils.

THE END.